numerology For nitwits

numerology For nitwits

Jil Balie

Writers Club Press
San Jose New York Lincoln Shanghai

numerology For nitwits

Writers Club Press
an imprint of iUniverse.com, Inc.

For information address:
iUniverse.com, Inc.
5220 S 16th, Ste. 200
Lincoln, NE 68512
www.iuniverse.com

ISBN: 0-595-15555-3

Printed in the United States of America

To my daughter Sally, who was smart enough to edit this book so well you really don't have to be a nitwit to understand it

Contents

1

A Number of Things

If you think it doesn't particularly matter what day you were born, you've probably never heard of numerology. If you have heard of it, chances are you dismissed it as being a weary little theory invented to amuse the simpleminded. This is a moot point. I feel the same way about calculus.

To put it simply, numerology identifies vibrations set into motion at the birth of *anything*—people, dogs, cats, events, whatever.

Then, by astutely studying these numbered vibrations, you can learn why you still run to fat no matter how many times you select a salad over french fries, never really understood your parents, and instantly fell in love with that scroungy little pooch at the S.P.C.A.

Pythagoras (whose name I studiously avoid trying to pronounce) was a Greek mathematician who took numerology to it's highest predictive levels. His system for defining numbers was so accurate it was eventually banned—kings didn't want to hear about possible defeats or the defection of one of their favorite Court cuties.

A little tact was obviously lacking since anyone caught using numerology was exiled or put to death.

Needless to say, numerology went into limbo for several hundred years, leaving no trace of Pythagoras' system except that he considered **28** to be the perfect number. Since there was no explanation, his reason remains a mystery. Was it the key to the universe or simply a new pal's telephone number?

In any event, as soon as the heat was off, numerology was revived and business was brisk with many systems being developed to unlock life's deepest secrets. The problem was finding the right system.

Fortunately, this buffet of arcane knowledge was soon reduced to a few dishes that people could take without getting indigestion. One popular "dish" simply assigned numbers **1** through **9** to the letters of the alphabet, repeating that formula as they progressed from A to Z until all 26 letters were used.

A more exotic "dish" is the Fadic system, developed by the ancient Chaldeans and Hebrews. In this one, letters of the alphabet are assigned numbers according to their vibrations with the exception of the number **9** which was considered to be the all-inclusive number of God and wasn't given to any letter.

Both of these systems have one thing in common: regardless of which one is used, the *interpretations* of the numbers are consistent.

The *big* difference is *how* these systems are used!

They can both be confidently used with birthday numbers—those unchanging numbers set into motion at the instant of the birth of anything. Unfortunately, this isn't true when it comes to using them to find your name number. And believe me, having the wrong name number is like Fred Astaire trying to tap dance in tennis shoes. The Fadic system was the only system I found that interprets the *name numbers* correctly.

I didn't come to this conclusion lightly.

By studiously pitting various numerology systems against each other—via every biography and obituary I could find—I finally came to the conclusion that what was good enough for the Chaldeans was good enough for me. (And, you, too!)

2

Who Says You Can't Take It with You?

You don't have to accept the theory of reincarnation in order to use numerology just as you don't have to be a computer whiz to use your word processor. But, in the words of the immortal Confucius—it helps.

When I speak of being born again, I'm not talking about getting tears in your eyes at the mention of Jesus and running around without wearing makeup. I'm talking about reincarnation. The theory of one body to a customer is just not logical.

There is an old Hindu saying (and I really don't know which old Hindu said it) that sums it up nicely. *"The Soul is the hand of God and the body is the glove."*

Not everyone is comfortable with the idea that they may have led previous lives. It could be depressing to think that after hanging around this old planet for at least several lifetimes, you're only digging ditches or taking orders at a drive-in window for hamburgers and fries.

It really is enough to make a person reject the whole idea!

But just be glad you are able to dig ditches or hand out the wrong fast-food order. There were previous incarnations when even the simplest tasks would have been beyond your ability or comprehension (and some maybe still are—like trying to get the cap off a bottle of aspirin.)

Each incarnation is like a grade in school. If you do your homework and pass all the tests, you get promoted to a higher level. If you don't pass the tests, you get to take the course over again (and again!) until you do pass. (Sound familiar?)

Now comes the good part: instead of getting gold stars or failing marks, you get KARMA!—*good* karma and *bad* karma.

Before we were born, most of us selected our parents, our name, and our birthday. Compare this to selecting a school and the courses you need (or think you need) to progress to a higher grade (or spiritual plane). Sometimes, after we settle in and start wrestling with a subject we don't understand (and haven't the foggiest intention of ever trying to use), the light begins to dawn. It occurs to us that—like many an optimistic student— in our eagerness to get started, we picked the wrong school, the wrong courses, and we aren't that happy with our teachers.

This can be a tricky situation, loaded with potential karma.

Some of us persevere, plodding along and doing the best we can. Others refuse to learn, hang out in the halls smoking, and crack a book only when threatened with actual mayhem. Little do these dopes know that those hated lessons will be waiting for them next time around!

Sometimes a genuine mistake has been made and what seemed like a good idea at the time turns out to be the worst decision since Adam decided to try a bite of that apple. When this happens, the *oversoul*—or real you which has survived all through those former lifetimes—kicks in and makes the decision as to whether you stay or go. This is to prevent further karma from being accumulated if you are unsuccessfully trying to cope with having the wrong birthday, wrong name, or wrong parents. (Please note: This doesn't mean you are in big trouble if you hate being born on Christmas day, prefer to be called Cynthia instead of Gertrude, and wish your parents were Meg Ryan and Tom Hanks.)

But, a word of caution: the decision to go or stay is not yours to make. The *oversoul* never recommends jumping off the Esperson building.

So, you better watch out, you better be nice—or you could spend a couple of lifetimes sidelined and wondering why nobody loves you.

Numerology and reincarnation work together like Fred and Ginger. One tells us what we came here to do and the other gives us the chance to do it better.

In our next lifetime, we may not "run to fat", be short, or be inclined to trip over anything bigger than a blade of grass.

3

Karma, Karma,
Who's Got the Karma?

Karma is a reaping of what has been sown in this and past lives.

There are two kinds of karma. Good karma (*Accumulative* karma) and bad karma (*Retributive* karma). Good karma shows up in the form of talents, good looks, happy life experiences, and nice legs. It is like a spiritual piggy bank; full of little coins of knowledge and good deeds you have been saving up since time began.

Bad karma, on the other hand, is like owing back taxes to the IRS—there is absolutely no way you're going to get off the hook. Repayment may be in the form of physical infirmities, total lack of social graces, rotten marriages, or bad breath.

In other words, you reap what you sow, harvest your own crops, and pay your own debts!

It's not difficult dealing with *good* karma. After all, who would object to having a life filled with goodies? It's having to cope with *bad* karma that can get really tacky.

Some souls facing a heavy karmic payoff might decide to get it over with in one lifetime by going "cold turkey". Kind of like a crash diet to get rid of all the weight—or karma—at once. These are the individuals who come into life with all the strikes against them and are dependent on the help and mercy of others. They may be lame, blind, mentally afflicted, poverty-ridden, or a Republican in a Democratic congress.

Cagier karmies who can't abide the thought of going through life without chocolate chip cookies, choose to pay off their karma (or lose that weight) in a more leisurely manner. Their lives will hold a measure of success and happiness, but also generous helpings of setbacks and a lifetime struggle to find jeans that fit.

Karma is often connected with other people: parents, children, relatives, and/or friends. This is *group* karma and all must work out their karmic problems together. If the people involved in group karma do not meet the challenge, they incur additional bad karma for themselves.

Remember: any knowledge you gain or skill you develop is yours to keep. As good karma is augmented and polished throughout ensuing lifetimes, it becomes perfect and—at the proper time— presents itself to the world under the name of Genius. This may help explain how tiny tots like Beethoven (just barely able to reach the harpsichord keys) compose music that is so dear to the heart of a dentist's waiting room.

We marvel at these prodigies, little knowing that we are adding—drop by drop—to our own personal *Accumulative Karma* (and ultimate geniuseness) by doggedly continuing to practice our piano scales, paint china, and write letters to the Editors.

If you are lolling beside your swimming pool while reading this, sipping sour mash Jack Daniels and wondering which Rolls to take on your shopping spree, chances are you did something right in a previous life (and are not a dope dealer or basketball player in this one). Maybe you did meet that millionaire at a Go-Go bar or Aunt Harriet died and left you all her Coca-Cola memorabilia, enabling you to finally get off welfare. In either case, you can be sure you've earned it. In one of your past lives, you sowed the seeds for this present day bounty. So enjoy!

On the other hand, if you happen to be in a hospital, encased up to your neck in a plaster cast, we may be dealing with *Retributive Karma*.

Karma travels in a circle, always returning to the one who originates it. Help a little old lady cross a busy street and you may later win the lottery. On the other hand, kick a dog on purpose—not just tripping over your pet that's snoozing in front of the refrigerator—and you could be a candidate for a much harder future "kick". The key word here is "Intent". You intended to *help* the little old lady (good karma) but wanted to *hurt* the doggie (bad karma with a kapital K.)

A load of bad karma such as that incurred by Hitler, can take several lifetimes to present itself for payment. In a situation like that, the soul will be in limbo until it gains the ability to redeem itself. Karmic debts *will* be paid. Murderers will suffer at the hands of their victims; the suicide will be pulled out of action in another life just when everything is going great; and the fun couple who use abortion as a means of birth control will spend several lifetimes longing for babies that never come.

It's how you handle your karma that counts.

We've all known people who became successful when everything seemed to be against them, while others—apparently destined for success—failed.

This is because the winners refused to passively accept whatever life handed them.

Abigail Abernathy (with the near-together eyes) became a star of Stage, Screen, and Television while Martha Feeney—in spite of having curly hair and the ability to recite *The Lady of Shalot*—worked as a clerk at Macy's for fifteen years without ever getting out of menswear.

Did Abigail ever think "my karma is too great for me to become the success I want to be"? I don't think so. Unlike many who can't tear themselves away from the TV except for trips to the fridge or to get another "Twinkie", she didn't use karma as an excuse to tidy up any misgivings about her life.

Abigail knew her eyes weren't her best feature but worked to overcome them (the bangs helped a lot.) Determined to get out from behind the counter at Barney's Beanery, she entered—and won—a local beauty contest. Parlaying a free trip to Hollywood and a small role in a bad movie into a movie contract, she became Lolita Lovely, and lived happily ever after.

Martha, on the other hand, should have added something to her repertoire besides *The Lady of Shalot*.

The main thing is to kwitchagripin' and go for it! Karma (good and bad) is a part of eveybody's life. It is something you work with—or around if need be—but it should never be used as an excuse for failure.

The whole purpose of karma is for the soul to learn the lessons it needs to know. This life is just as important as any other one you have ever lived so make it count! Remember, you do have free will (which is why you have karma).

So, you better watch out, you better be nice—or you could spend a couple of lifetimes sidelined and wondering why nobody loves you.

4

Your Number and What It Means

Some numerologists believe that your name number is the number you should be identified by.

Not so.

The day you were born is the significant number because this number is fixed and unchangeable—unlike the numbers of your name which *can* be changed.

If you were born on October 3rd you are a **3**; August **8**th, an **8**; September **18**th, a **9** (**1+8=9**); and so on.

As you can see, in numerology, numbers are always reduced to a single digit. However, by identifying them as an **18-9** (or **16-7, 23-5, 24-6** etc.), you know what kind of a **9** (or **7, 5,** or **6** etc.) you are dealing with. Compound numbers (double digits) add emphasis to the basic number's vibration.

The name number is important, but your birthday number tells us exactly who—and what—you are!

So, without further ado, here are the definitions of numbers **1** through **9,** with all the multiple numbers therein.

5

Ones

People born on the 1st, 10th, 19th, or 28th of the month

Anyone born on a **1** day is positive, creative, and determined. Born leaders, they can organize a project quicker than you can say "Something has to be done about those gooney birds!" Thanks to the **1**s, those gooney birds are in the bag. (Oops!)

Princess Di (July **1**) certainly demonstrated these qualities in her various crusades against AIDs, landmines, and bores. Although one publication referred to her as "a concerned tourist", this did not prevent her from going to places so scary, most people would have called in with a sick headache.

1s do not linger over a project. (Maybe all those in congressional investigating committees should be **1**s!) And, whether a **1** is saving the gooney birds or decorating the Sistine Chapel, it will be done quickly and efficiently. This may explain why it took Michelangelo ten years to paint the Sistine Chapel—he wasn't born on a **1** day.

The **1** is a root number. Being the base of all numbers, it usually has no trouble adapting to any other number—unless that number is the **4.** The **4** is a karmic link to a past life (or lives) of the **1** and is roughly akin to a magnet coming across a piece of iron—zap! Try and separate them! The **1-4** relationship always involves an unresolved issue from a former life. For this reason, a **1** will often have to cope with a **4** child, mate, relative, or "Boss".

At this point, I would like to say that it is good for *all* numbers to know as much about the **1** as possible. It may not keep you from contemplating hari-kari while trying to cope with that **1** in your life, but you will at least understand *why!*

1s are extremely sensitive to criticism and will not accept any form of it lightly, treating the offender to a sulk that could last for days—or until the error of the criticizer way is remedied.

Interestingly enough, they can be very critical of others, astutely picking out a flaw at twenty paces on a foggy day.

Fortunately, their great sense of humor keeps things (and friends) in balance. I don't mean to imply that a **1** starts telling little jokes about the Rabbi and the Pope while reading you the riot act, I just mean that most of the time they can see something funny in any situation—even one that concerns them—and laugh about it.

The most important thing to know about a **1** is to *never offer them advice!* This will be construed as telling them what to do! No, no, no, no, and no! Do *not* do this.

If you are quietly observing a **1** determinedly trying to pull open a door that is plainly marked "Push", say nothing unless it can be put into a casual remark: "Perhaps this door was accidentally installed backwards."

Never say: "Good Gosh, Dora! PUSH, don't PULL!"

The first remark allows the **1** to decide on their own that a change is required. The second will inspire the **1** to rip the door off its hinges.

Tact is their middle name and this is good because they are super critical. Being perfectionists, they have little sympathy for anything less than perfect. Shopping with a **1** is an exercise in controlled hysteria; they will examine every thing a shopping mall has to offer— never hesitating to call for a "higher authority" if things aren't up to snuff. This insures meeting a lot of new people—from the floor manager to the head of the department store.

A **1** will endure any hardship to attain success. Believing whole heartedly that money *does* buy happiness, they will work until they drop in order to get their hands on it.

The word "indefatigable" was invented to describe a **1**!

If there is a **1** in your life, consider yourself lucky because life will never be dull.

The Meaning of Your Particular 1 Birthday

1

A person born on the first day of the month exhibits all the inherent traits of a **1**. Perseverance (or tenacity) enables this number to look beyond defeat of any kind to reach their goals. They push to achieve but will walk that extra mile to help someone else (or a cause).

1s often have lonely childhoods but make up for it as soon as they discover the nearest shopping mall or Starbucks. Attachments are formed with lightning speed and kept—unless the friend disappoints them one time too many, then it's over.

Any willfulness they may exhibit really stems from a sense of inferiority (shhh, don't tell *them*!) This is in their own minds because they demand perfection—not only in others—but in themselves.

10-1

This **1** is intensified and their talents and skills are often remarkable! They may be the best ukelele player on the block or the best president of the United States but, whatever they are, they are always RIGHT—so don't argue with 'em.

All of the aforementioned attributes of the **1** apply to this **10-1**—maybe even more so. They generally have more than one iron in the fire, hedging their bets by developing other skills—in case they tire of taking orders from someone who doesn't know half as much as they do.

Happily, tact, likability, and a sweet disposition generally prevails.

19-1

The **19-1** is generally regarded as a number of success and happiness. This is if they can decide what they really want; they have a hard time making up their minds. Not making it any easier is a do-it-again side to this number. This isn't bad if you really enjoyed doing whatever it was the first time—like being elected President of the United States. (Bill Clinton, Aug. **19**)

Their biggest problem is restlessly changing jobs, mates, etc. Wyatt Earp (Mar.**19**) spent only seventeen months in Tombstone, Arizona, before going on to various other careers. What he did before Tombstone—or after—isn't generally known except that for a little while he was a newspaper reporter (imagine not giving *him* a story!)

28-1

Did I mention that Pythagoras, the great granddaddy of numerology, decreed **28-1** as *the* perfect number? Capable, witty, artistic, clever, and tireless, the bearers of this number are also Ace shopaholics.

Similar to the **19-l,** the **28-1** brings several distinctively different lifestyles. Jacqueline Kennedy Onassis (July **28**) had an interesting job resume: Debutante, Roving Newspaper Reporter, Senator's Wife, First Lady, Widow, Billionaire's Wife, and Editor of Artistic Books.

Incidentally, Jay Leno (Apr. **28**) demonstrates the back and forth tendency of the number every time he comes on stage to do his monologues. He immediately takes one step forward, then one step backward; one step forward then one step backward; one step...etc.

6

Twos

People born on the 2nd, 11th, 20th, or 29th of the month

2s are the peace lovers of the world! Always pleasant, they prefer that others make the hard decisions. If, however, push comes to shove, the **2** will step in and get the job done.

Many doctors, lawyers, nurses, teachers, politicians, and scientists have the **20-2** prominent in their number-scope. This number stands for service to others. It has been said that if a presidential candidate doesn't have the **20-2** in their name or birthday, they either won't be elected or will be a rotten president.

Of course, there are always exceptions to the rule— any rule. Some of our best presidents didn't have a shred of a **20-2** in their numbers. Abraham Lincoln, Feb **12**, for instance. On the other hand, Bill Clinton, Aug.**19**, had **20-2**s all over the place. Go figure.

In money matters, they are generally careful but a **2** can spot a bargain a mile off. Unfortunately, after saving $10.00 on a pair of antique Eurasian snow shoes, the **2** will turn round and lend five times that much to good old Uncle Ralph who plans to get a job someday.

History reeks with **2**s who contributed generously to a good cause. Marie Antoinette (Nov. **2**) persuaded hubby, King Louis XVI, to spend thousands of francs to help that new upstart country, America, when it needed it the most. Thanks to her, money, supplies, and warm bodies to fight the British helped us to create our own taxes!

Revolutions don't come cheap—as she later discovered!

Did I mention that **2**s are very intrepid?

Their biggest problem is overcoming a restless tendency. They can become bored very quickly. Their second biggest problem is allowing others to dominate them. (Maybe they prefer that to being bored.)

Strangely enough, some **2**s can work in isolation and *not* be bored. Work environments that would send other numbers up the wall, are ignored by them. Maybe this is why they make such good scientists; teeny little cubicles in labs don't bother them at all!

Trusting in love affairs, a **2** can easily be led down the garden path—if they aren't doing the leading. It follows that they can be the world's most faithful companions—or dedicated femme fatales and womanizers. It seems to depend on what kind of a **2** they are. The **2** is usually *Old Dog Trey*; The **11-2** is usually too busy to do anything but work or take aspirins for that chronic headache or sniffle. The **20-2** may be out to save the world but they can always find time for a little hanky-panky if it presents itself, and the **29-2 is** an almost insatiable flirt.

2s are good employers and/or employees because they are efficient, conscientious, and fair minded. They will bend over backward to see the other fella's side. However, If they are mistaken for being pushovers, there could be a nasty shock. Their revenge is quiet, subtle, but very effective.

All in all, the peace loving 2s make the world a better place in which to live (just ask Uncle Ralph).

The Meaning of Your Particular 2 Birthday

2

A person born on the second day of the month is easy going and cheerful—even with people who try to take advantage of them. They want everybody to love 'em and will go to great lengths to keep people on their side. This doesn't apply to those who nag or depress them— good advice for *any* number!

Interestingly, they get along especially well with other 2s. Bing Crosby (May 2) hit the road many times with Bob Hope (May 29) and he and Irving Berlin (born May 11), practically made *White Christmas* a national anthem.

2s can be determined, even obstinate, when it comes to something they want to do but they will always listen to reason.

11-2

The main purpose of this number is to push the bearer toward success. It also brings hurty backs and addictions (this 2 must never light up that first cigarette. They can become addicted to almost any substance except spinach.)

Designated as a Master Number (the other one is the 22-4), it either masters you or you master it! The two 1s

(**11**) bring traits of the **1** and account for their ability to hang in there and get things done. Where would we be if Thomas Edison (Feb.**11**) had not been so tenacious in his quest to invent our electricity bill?

20-2

Many politicians, doctors, lawyers, beauticians, and ambulance drivers have this **20-2** in their numberscope because this number wants to serve others.

This particular **2** craves companionship and seeks jobs that involve having people around them. It is an unhappy **20-2** who has to work alone. They would be happier being a front man for the mob or working in Madame Kinky's House of Joy (even if they made less money) than finding themselves in a cubicle, facing a computer everyday or alone at home making the same old bed.

No matter what the circumstances, if they are handed a job to do, they do it efficiently (even if their minds are elsewhere—probably plotting their getaway!)

29-2

The vibrations of this number give new meaning to perpetual motion. It also denotes a karmic disability or addiction.

The *good* part is the absolute charm, cuteness, talent, ability to get along with just about anybody in the world, and generosity that puts Santa Claus to shame!

I may as well mention that there is also a tendency to put on weight by just *sniffing* a doughnut!

This number easily attracts eager minions to its side.

To be perfectly honest, it also attracts just about every germ known to mankind. (The ideal spouse for a **29-2** is a doctor!)

7

Threes

People born on the 3rd, 12th, 21st, or 30th of any month

For those born on a **3** day, optimism reigns. No matter how wretched the circumstances, a **3** can always manage to see the good side. Pollyanna, the "Glad Girl", may well have been a **3**.

Their self-confidence helps them overcome adversity in astonishing ways. A natural leader, they are astute in the ways of business and can quickly rise to a position of leadership. But, no matter how busy they are, they will still take time to play the guitar, whip up that cartoon, or write a book. (Did I mention that these people are invariably talented?)

Books, books, and more books occupy their time and their hobbies are usually on the creative side—accompanied by music (they will have the largest CD collection in the neighborhood.)

A love of physical activity leads many **3**s into vigorous sports. They'll ski, play tennis, swim, ride horses, bulls, or motorcycles. If a little thing like a broken kneecap (or head) happens, it is generally ignored until treatment is convenient and fits into their schedule (or they pass out!)

Never give a **3** an ultimatum. It will either be ignored or they will do just the opposite of what is expected. This is because they are their own masters.

They are wonderful friends. If you've got a problem, they will try to help you solve it. If you need a shoulder to cry on, they will offer theirs. If you need money, they will point you in the direction of the nearest money-lender.

Big problems seldom defeat **3**s but they are inclined to fret about small ones—worrying is one of their favorite pastimes. This doesn't prevent them from being a bit dictatorial; they not only want to be in control, they expect others to *like* being told what to do.

Independent and proud, a **3** dislikes being obligated to anyone—be it Mom, Dad, Wife, or Boss. They also hate being limited in any area; they want to do what they want when they want the way they want to do it. (Did I mention they can be just the teensiest bit selfish?)

Their rationale is simple: if someone is going to be unhappy, it's not going to be me.

Well, why not?

The Meaning of Your Particular 3 Birthday

3

This **3** needs to guard against being judgmental. Few mere mortals can measure up to their expectations—or to them. But they can also be so tactful, the target of their barbs might even thank them for pointing out their short comings.

Their interests are wide but they grow bored quickly and seek new amusements to ward off ennui. Sometimes their amusements can be a tad worrisome; they like to take risks and the rougher the sport (or higher the stakes) the better they like it.

On the other hand, they can amuse themselves even if alone on a desert island. Or married. Many a spouse of the **3** grows accustomed to playing solitaire.

12-3

Those who have this number are able to attract just about anyone—or thing—they want. Usually very attractive, they are also clever in money matters. This brings them to the attention of some who want what they have, even to the point of plotting to get it.

Their main forte is to enjoy life—if the tendency to fret over trifles is overcome—but they mustn't allow others to manipulate them. Abraham Lincoln (Feb.12) was happy being a country lawyer until he finally achieved the goals his wife, Mary Todd, set for him. Although he kept losing elections, she goaded him on until he became President of the United States. ("Be careful what you wish for!")

21-3

This **3** stands for brilliant success after a long series of trials. The trick is to still be standing when all that "brilliant success" arrives!

The fact that the **2** leads off may account for it; they find themselves being told what to do by others until they finally start managing their own affairs. When that happens, stand back: this **3** is dynamic!

Talented, there will be a piano, guitar, or flute nearby or a pair of tap shoes. While not as "bubbly" as some of the Other **3**s, this one brightens up a room just by coming into it because a little aura of sunshine always seems to hover over them.

The **21-3** brings many rewards but this **3** will have to work for them. If you don't believe me, just ask Queen Elizabeth II! (Apr. **21**)

30-3

A thoughtful, mental number, this **3** can handle detail work easily. They also have good communication skills and are excellent teachers, actors, insurance agents, or politicians.

The **30-3** has the ability to continue with a project long beyond the realm of good sense. Vincent Van Gogh (Mar. **30**) kept right on painting although he could never sell his pictures. (Today you would have to be a basketball star to own one.)

A tendency toward depression should be nipped in the bud—new plans or goals are there for the taking. If health problems crop up, the **30-3** is usually able to recuperate faster than Superman can leap across tall buildings—or find the nearest phone booth!

8

Fours

People born on the 4th, 13th, 22nd, or 31st of any month

Enthusiastic to the point of exhausting other lesser numbers, **4**s start out expecting the world to be their oyster—but the "pearl" is usually just a grain of sand. This doesn't deter any of them in the least. No matter how disagreeable events may be, they are just as happy as if they were millionaires (and many are!)

On the other hand, the word "taciturn" might have been coined to describe a **4**. Then again, there is probably too much lighthearted frolicking going on in the world. The only thing wrong with this picture is that the **4**s could be doing all the frolicking.

These are not demonstrative people. If a **4** glances in your direction, lets his eyes meet yours for 20 seconds, then smiles (just barely) before going back to doing whatever he was doing, you have received an almost hysterical expression of their interest.

Always talented (especially those born on the **13**th) they are also rebels. Maybe not in the sense of Fidel Castro (who, incidentally, *is* a **13-4**) but they are definitely on the side of the underdog. If they believe that something is unfair or discriminatory, they are determined to seek justice. The weird part is that although they can find justice for others, they seldom can find it for themselves.

A natural fall guy, they may simply be a bystander to wrong doing but will get the blame. A typical example is the **4** who stopped a thief from stealing a tire off a car. Then, while putting the tire back on, *he* was arrested!

Fate is capricious where **4**s are concerned so don't try predicting anything for them. When a perfectly normal, predictable outcome is expected—and those expectations are based on logical facts—forget it! That nice, predictable outcome will probably make a 180° turn and run the **4** down! (**4**s aren't called one of the *Playthings of Destiny* for nothing!)

Recognizing that certain karmic lessons have to be learned (or karmic debts paid), **4**s seem to unerringly select the school of Hard Knocks. Fortunately, they have built-in reserves of determination and perseverance that help them cope with their karmic lessons.

A **4** never hesitates to take the opposite side of an argument and seems to enjoy alienating people by being unconventional (the key word here is " alien"—I often think **4**s are from another planet.) This can cause hostile reactions among acquaintances (and sometimes mere passersby) and provides the **4** with a ready supply of enemies who are tickled to death to work against him. This can be the source of a great deal of loneliness— unless another **4** comes along.

Curiously, **1**s and **4**s always seem to find each other. You might call them karma magnets—with the karmic debt being on the side of the **4.** Surprisingly, they can be a devoted team.

If **4**s believe in a cause, they will win or go down fighting for it. The "hippie" movement of the '60s was probably started by a **4** and maintained by a host of eager little **4**s—all long haired, beaded, and equipped with flowers and guitars, ready to burn their draft cards (or bras) at the drop of a comb.

A sharp sense of humor (usually) allows them to see the funny side of an otherwise distressing situation. (Some **4**s seem to laugh a lot.)

Naturally courageous, they happily leap in where angels fear to tread. In 1927 (long before people were crammed into a small cylinder called the *Concorde* and shot across the ocean), Charles Lindbergh (Feb. **4**) flew the Atlantic ocean alone in a single engine plane without even a parachute or something to read!

Precise in thinking, a **4** does a job throughly, no matter how tedious. Right now, there are back rooms, cubicles, and outposts filled with **4**s who make their living by filing canceled checks, stocking grocery shelves, reading reams of statistics, or studying lists of rotten movies in order to program just the right ones to frustrate viewers looking for a little entertainment.

Meticulous attention to detail is good, but **4**s mustn't lose sight of the larger goals. A good example is someone who cleans and polishes, empties the ashtray as soon as the first ash falls, spreads newspapers on newly washed floors, and waxes the garbage pail. Then, while happily plucking a piece of lint (invisible to the naked eye) from the pristine carpet, their mate is quietly easing out the door—headed for a cozy evening with that slob down the street who could not care less whether the garbage pail is waxed—or even if there *is* a garbage pail!

4s make changes reluctantly and then only after much agonizing thought. But, once a decision is made, it will take an act of God (or Congress) to budge them from their chosen course.

Generally steadfast in marriage, the 4 can make a few false starts but eventually get it right. Invariably, the partner is from a former lifetime. This can bring about a union fraught with problems or a marriage that zings along reaping piles of goodies—or both. For those who are finally ready to settle down, another 4 can be a safe harbor.

The Meaning of Your Particular 4 Birthday

4

Extraordinarily talented, those born on a 4 day are optimistic and have a happy-go-lucky nature. When things are going smoothly, they're fun to be around. If things aren't going so smoothly, morose and moody take on new meanings. Although a loyal friend, 4s tend to repeat mistakes in relationships—and the second time around isn't any easier. Try and curb your enthusiasm concerning new projects until you have all the facts; going off half-cocked is a sure way to failure.

13-4

The Ancients said this number represented the *Chosen One of God.* It got a bad reputation because the true Easter is April 15th which makes *Good Friday* the 13th. (Have you noticed that disasters seem to happen on "Good Friday"—the San Francisco Earthquake, Lincoln's Assassination, the sinking of the Titanic...) The important thing to remember is: if used for good, the **13-4** is a lucky number.

This number brings multiple talents. It also indicates karmic tests have been passed—but this is final exam time! Don't screw up or you'll just have to try, try again until you get it right. Bummer.

If other **4**s are in your numberscope, you were probably a very powerful individual in another life—and can be very powerful in this one! (I wonder who Thomas Jefferson, Apr.**13**, was in *his* former life? And who he is now?)

22-4

This is the other *Master Number* in numerology (the first one being the **11-2**). While enjoying most of the attributes of the **4**s mentioned, unusual things happen to a **22-4** because it is a number of delusion and these **4**s look at life through rose colored glasses.

Preferring to *always* believe the best in people, this trusting **4** is left wide open to be taken to the cleaners— and it won't be just to get their clothes pressed! If you have this birthday, check out that sure-fire investment before you hand over all of your money to someone who has a car waiting at the curb with the motor running.

31-4

This number is not noted for hilarity. Their motto seems to be "Lets be frank and earnest" (Okay, you be Frank and I'll be Ernest.)

Strong willed (another term for obstinate), they set goals and doggedly pursue them to completion. Just don't get in their way.

Because they are afraid of poverty there is almost always a savings account tucked away and they usually spend their money very carefully. But, if someone is in need, they are first to open up their wallets.

They may be careful but they're not misers.

9

Fives

People born on the 5th, 14th, or 23rd of any month

"Give me liberty or give me death" could have been spoken by a **5** because they love their freedom. It follows that they hate to be pinned down as to time, place, or dates.

If a **5** goes out for the paper and doesn't return for three days, don't ask why. If they want you to know where they were, they will tell you—maybe. This is true regarding *any* question to a **5** such as "When are you coming home?", "Will you call me when you arrive?" or "How old are you?" (Just kidding—this is a question no one should ask anybody unless you are talking to a toddler.)

Their aversion to being pinned down might be because they are *Quickly Returning Souls*.

These are people whose lives were cut short in their previous incarnation and they got back as soon as they could—not waiting the usual ninety years or so on the *other* side.

Many times, they are born to older parents and will be an only child (the **23-5** is especially suspect.)

Because they are out of sync with their regular incarnation circle, they will love but not really know their parents, siblings, or spouses.

Interestingly, they always have friends who are much older than they—people who are the age they would have been had their previous life not been interrupted. They also like old movies, music with lyrics (hard to find these days), and feel that the only place to show everything you've got is in the privacy of your home— not at the super market.

The next time you see or hear of a May-December romance, it could be that one of them is a **5**—just doing what they would have done in their previous lifetime.

A **5** seldom lingers over the past. In fact, they don't linger over the present—or anywhere—or for anyone! Quick-witted, impulsive, and magnetic, they make friends easily and get along with almost everybody. But, it's almost always "easy come, easy go".

Because it's a volatile number, changes come quickly—right out of the blue, so to speak. For this reason, **5**s must heed their astrological sign. If a *fire* sign, they must be careful around fire (Aries, Leo, Sagittarius); if a *water* sign, wear water wings (Pisces, Cancer, Scorpio); if an *earth* sign watch out for collisions, heights and explosions (Taurus, Virgo, Capricorn); and, if an *air sign,* fly only if they feel good about it (Aquarius, Gemini, Libra)

Great bursts of enthusiasm and equally great bursts of despondency are theirs (talk about your mood swings!)

They also have a temper. Woe unto the target of a **5**'s rage (fortunately they don't rile easily.)

Whether deciding to be a statesman or hairdresser, **5**s should consider choices carefully. You don't know what unhappiness is unless you've been around a frustrated **5**. They would put Henry VIII to shame!

I hope this clear, logical explanation of a **5** helps. If it does, will somebody explain it to me?

The Meaning of Your Particular 5 Birthday

5

To be really happy, this **5** needs to have people around, especially in work. Roy Rogers, Nov **5**, came from a family of farmers who ate regularly. He, however, preferred singing with his little band of musicians—and starving. It's not surprising that as soon as he became *King of the Cowboys* (which, I suppose, made *Trigger* a Prince) he opened up a fast food chain.

Speaking of money, it can become an obsession with a **5**. The fear of driving a Ford instead of a Bentley could be the motivating factor, but amassing assets could become almost a game. The trick is to not lose sight of other, more important things—like learning to tap-dance or play the ukelele.

14-5

Changes *really* come without warning for this **5**! They also have flashbacks from babyhood until their early teens. These can be unsettling (not many people can laugh off recurring visions of falling, drowning, or wearing brown shoes at the prom). Many believe they might be seeing their future death (or a major faux pax) but this isn't so. These flashbacks occur because their previous passing was fairly recent, as well as traumatic. Incidentally, birthmarks are said to indicate the site of the fatal wound. Interesting? (And no, I don't know what it means if you have a birthmark in the shape of a rose on your derriere.)

23-5

This is a "power" number that promises success and help from others. It has all characteristics of the **5** but is helped considerably by the gentle **2** and the darling little **3** which is like adding curls to Shirley Temple. Speaking of which: Shirley is a **23-5** (Apr. **23**), born to middle-aged parents who already had two half-grown sons.

These **5**s can be outstanding successes or embarrassing failures. Doing things halfway just never seems to occur to them. A number of achievement, the **23-5** seems able to do it all (unless they have the IQ of a gnat—in which case they can go into politics.)

The only thing I would suggest is that **23-5**s be kind to us lesser mortals without such dynamic vibrations! (Mainly because we're the ones who can't wait to vote for you!)

10

Sixes

People born on the 6th, 15th, or 24th of any month

Children born on a **6** day can be holy terrors—absolutely determined to have their own way! Docile as an angel at times, they will turn right around and give the cat a bath in the toilet.

Punishment is a waste of time. You can try reasoning; forbidding TV programs (if you can find one for children that doesn't feature mayhem short of actual gang warfare); or refusing to order pizza for supper. None of the above works—but praise and cuddling might.

This doesn't mean the cat won't get another toilette in the toilet, but at least there could be a pause for reflection before the cat is dunked.

Happily, these children usually grow up to be charming, witty, and good companions and when they have children of their own, they will spoil them rotten. I guess this is nature's way of proving that what goes around, comes around!

Adjustment is another word that describes a **6.** This may be because they are perfectionists and are constantly adjusting things to make them perfect. (They could be the ideal chiropractor.)

Show Biz, as well as politics, is a natural milieu because their communication skills are marvelous! Ronald Reagan (Feb.**6**) parlayed sports announcing into making movies into being President of the United States.

One of the more important things a **6** should consider is that other people have ideas, goals, desires, and agendas of their own. The fact that a **6** is convinced that (s)he—and (s)he alone—is right doesn't cut it with most people. In fact, if anything it will send them reeling off into the night! Present your plans, etc., then pay attention to reasons why they are not accepted—if that's the case—but don't try to bulldoze your way through, anyway. This is not a pretty sight.

If they start worrying about their health, they can be super-hypochondiacs, spotting a potential germ at forty Paces. This can turn them into reclusive hermits, living alone at the top of a mountain with all the windows sealed. Well, maybe this is an exaggeration but then again...

They have to avoid expounding so enthusiastically on a favorite topic that most of their audience—family, co-workers, guests, dog—have quietly left by way of Albuquerque. They'll return, of course, because a **6** is so magnetic. The bottom line is: If a **6** is unattached it's because they want it that way.

The Meaning of Your Particular 6 Birthday

6

This **6** has to know they are appreciated! Sensitive to beauty and drama, they are often a shining star. Their only problem is knowing when to leave the spotlight and letting someone else have a shot at twinkling.

Social, tactful, and born arbitrators, they are good people to have around in case of a disagreement—if they are on *your* side.

Their love of beauty is reflected in everything they do. If you see a Mercedes-Benz convertible tooling down the road with a pair of fuzzy pink dice dangling from the rear-view mirror, the driver is not a **6**; otherwise, the dice would have been ermine.

15-6

This number has a special magnetism of its own and is a lucky number even if people don't say "Come on **6**!" when they roll a pair of dice.

Able to coax just about anything they want out of anybody, they will always try to have their way. Unfortunately, if they don't get it, they are capable of being extremely unpleasant. Hopefully, these tantrums won't last too long (some have been known to hold a grudge for years)

Did I mention that sometimes they are very determined?

Note: if there is an **8** name in the numberscope, there could be an element of "black magic" present. However, don't be alarmed—unless there is an overwhelming urge to make a few voodoo dolls!

24-6

This **24-6** has a practical approach to life. If there is a job to be done, they get it done—but they will always receive the assistance they need in doing it. Similar to the **23-5**s, people just naturally want to do things for them. This may account for so many marrying "rich", inheriting fortunes, or winning the lottery.

Happily, they're not stingy.

The only thing I would suggest is that they not be too dogmatic about what *they* think is the right thing to do.

11

Sevens

People born on the 7th, 16th, or 25th of the month

Show me a **7** and I will show you someone who has absolutely no interest in the occult—or is so psychic, they're almost scary! There is no happy medium (well, some "mediums" are pretty happy). But whether or not they believe in outside forces, if a **7** mentions they dreamed Cousin Bertram was coming for a visit, you'd better spruce up that spare room (or cancel the paper and leave town).

7s are just as interesting when it comes to religion. Some are cavalier about it to the point of ennui while others become almost rabid about their convictions. But if a **7** is not happy with their church options, they, like Mary Baker Eddy (July **16**th), create their own! When she grew disgruntled with the church she had attended all her life, she created Christian Science.

7s can be outstanding writers and artists. When you combine those skills with their clairvoyance, you get someone like the marvelously talented Rose O'Neill (June **25**) who created the immortal little *Kewpies* to illustrate her children's stories. She said she had a dream one night and saw the adorable little creatures all around her. They even told her their name was "Kewpie". These elfin characters became the rage in the 1920's and now *Kewpie* dolls have become such collector items that you would have to be Bill Gates to afford one!

The **7** has a mystical aura that seems to straddle the chasm of time. They are as comfortable in the past as they are in the present. Mystery is their second nature.

7s care little about material things—money isn't the be-all and end-all that seems to drive other numbers so hard. Even so, they can become rich through their keen sense of business and originality. Their main problem is persevering—many **7**s drop by the wayside just before they finally reach that pot of gold at the end of the rainbow.

A **7** will either marry early or maybe not at all. One of the problems might be that this number can become so analytical that it will bypass perfectly good partners. Suitors with a million dollars could be rejected because they wears white socks with suits (actually, as far as I'm concerned, this *is* a valid reason for staying single and collecting homeless cats.) Whatever the situation, **7**s can be just as happy single—maybe happier.

Non-conforming, the **7**s form their own opinions and will think, act, and dress the way they want. They make friends slowly but keep them forever. Maybe that's because gossip is a no-no—with a **7**, the Muck stops there!

Patience, ability to endure hardships (even unto shopping in a crowded mall), and a mega curiosity about life, are specialties of the **7**. Marie Curie (Nov. **7**) lived during a time when women fit in nicely with the wood-work but she still managed to discover radium (or was that uranium? I must try and catch that Greer Garson movie again.)

The Meaning of Your Particular 7 Birthday

7

7s don't realize just how smart they are—rather like the Straw Man in "The Wizard of Oz". He was desperate to get a brain but had already solved most of the problems encountered on "The Yellow Brick Road".

Preferring a rural setting to an urban one, solitude to crowds, a good book to watching TV, these 7s have a passion for the simple life but can adapt to the fast lane if life demands it.

Travel to faraway places is a favorite thing but if there is a large body of water nearby, it'll do nicely, thank you.

16-7

The number is indicative of a karmic payoff. The 16-7 will build you up and then—ha, ha—pull the rug out from under you.

These 7s cling to what (or who) is theirs and can pursue goals doggedly. Sometimes their attitude is: what is mine is mine and what is *yours* is probably mine, too. So watch it. Be fair.

But they do share big time.

Mary Baker Eddy (July 16) gave us Christian Science and Ginger Rogers (ditto July 16th) gave us Fred Astaire.

Incidentally, John Phillip Sousa and W.C.Handy were both born on Nov. **16**. Sousa wrote The *Stars and Stripes Forever* which practically became this country's national anthem.

W.C.Handy wrote The *St.Louis Blues* which many thought *was* the national anthem!

25-7

These are the travelers of the world. Fortunately, languages come easily to most of them. This guarantees they can order lunch no matter what country they're visiting. They love the finer things in life but must be careful that "gourmet" doesn't change into "gourmand".

My main advice is to put down that travel folder for a second and let other people know what you're thinking from time to time. Just don't overdo it. Because they can become fanatics on just about any subject that interests them, they should avoid discussing religion, politics, in-laws, or chocolate chip cookies.

12

Eights
People born on the 8th, 17th, or 26th of any month

There should be an organization like Alcoholics Anonymous for people who are **8**s. ("Hello! My name is Jil and I was born on an **8** day.")

If *you* were born on an **8** day, I suggest that you get yourself a nice hot cup of coffee and sit down before reading any further. Even if your life has already demonstrated that roller-coasters aren't limited to theme parks, you are now going to find out *why*. (A little background music, please—violins will do nicely.)

Called *Playthings of Destiny*, fate is so capricious with these numbers that only an idiot would try to predict for them. This is because of the karma attached to an **8** making it one of the mystery numbers of numerology (the other is the **4**).

Often combining *Good Karma* and *Bad Karma* in equally generous helpings, people born on an **8** day can be surprising. Harry Truman (May **8**) is the only President of the United States born on an **8** day.

And Elvis Presley was born on Jan. **8**.

A tie salesman and the son of dirt-poor parents changed the world as we know it. Harry brought in the atomic age and Elvis gave us Rock and Roll!

Some karmies aren't ready to handle being an **8.** When that happens, they use their *out clause* and leave, often coming back to the same family (unless the family was part of the problem), with an easier birthday (the oversoul determines this, not you.)

Because the **8** is one of the weirdest numbers in numerology, it's wise to avoid emphasis on its vibration. Like tip-toeing through the graveyard on Halloween, there's no point in calling attention to yourself with all those spooks hanging around!

So what can you do about it?

Here are a few suggestions. They are not guaranteed to work but could make life a little easier. And, remember, there really are no rules for an **8** (Harry Truman proved that.)

If you are using a name that adds up to a **4** (that other karmic mystery number), you might want to think about changing the spelling or even take a new name.

Try not to live in a house whose numbers add up to a **4.** (Remember I said the same thing about a **4** living in an **8** house.)

In other words, try not to cross the **8s** with the **4s.**

Now for some of the good stuff.

8s never do anything halfway. If they are religious they practically walk on water; if not, they consider Sunday to be the best day of the week to really catch up on their sleep and the funny papers.

Most have wills of iron, self-discipline, and determination. Their slogan seems to be "The impossible just takes a little longer." Others of us feel that all of the above leaves little room for fun and relaxation. I agree with Scarlett O'Hara that "after all, tomorrow is another day."

Outspoken and often critical of others, mediocrity drives them over the edge and is dealt with by sharp, precise condemnation. The problem is, they just don't understand that other numbers are not as generously endowed with inborn abilities to get things done.

Pity.

An **8** may appear to be aloof but nothing could be farther from the truth. Many have to be careful they don't dominate the party scene. At a social gathering, you may find an **8** tap dancing on the coffee table, but another **8** could be curled up in a corner somewhere. This is because some fear rejection and have difficulty expressing emotion (or we're just resting after doing our imitation of Judy Garland or Elvis.)

8s attract others easily—finding a friend is no problem; it's keeping them that eludes an **8.**

Where there is an **8** you will most likely find a **9**. This is karma, karma, and more karma! Since it is always a past relationship from a former incarnation, woe betide the **8** who doesn't resolve any difficulty it presents. Next time around, the problem will re-present itself.

Because they are generous, they will share any or all of their good ideas, abilities, money, and hard work. The sad part is, many who take from an **8** seldom return their generosity.

Oh, well, no good deed ever goes unpunished—nor does an **8**!

The Meaning of Your Particular 8 Birthday

8

This is a business and financial number (or so they would have you believe.) The commercial world could be your natural habitat—or the zoo (remember, we're talking about **8**s here!) You have no trouble coming up with original concepts that can bring great wealth, fame, and acclaim—to *others*. Try and work out a game plan where some of that loot sticks to you.

Other than that, you do have a pretty good sense of humor, special talents and abilities from your former lives, and an abiding distrust of all kissy-kissy people, including distant relatives and politicians.

17-8

This number denotes fame and fortune. This doesn't mean everyone born on the **17**th of the month is going to be rich and famous; it does mean that—in your own orbit and according to your own efforts—you will stand out. (You could be known as the best ukelele player in town!)

Dynamic and independent, these **8**s refuse to take a back seat to anyone but can be defensive to the point of despondency if they are thwarted—they do not take criticism lightly. Fortunately, many are noted for their unusual good looks so what's there to criticize?

Their main goal usually is to find someone who understands them.

Sometimes, they do.

26-8

A dynamic number that is super susceptible to deception. After working hard to make a little nest-egg, the **26-8**s allow the fox to come in and enjoy an omelet!

All of the attributes of the **8** are in this number but they are hampered by wrong choices. Wanting to always believe the best in people, finding not only a ray but a veritable spotlight of hope in almost impossible situations, and being optimistic to the point of being imbecilic, just leads this **8** out onto the precipice, where they happily enjoy the view!

The bottom line for the **26-8** is to not be a gullible traveler!

13

Nines

People born on the 9th, 18th, or 27th of any month

9s are determined, persistent, heroic, adamant, private, and fighters. (If provoked, they can reach a boiling point in 30 seconds or less, then pow!—"to the moon, Alice!")

Intuition and emotion seem to be their guiding forces and their assessments of people, situations, or events are right on target. Logic is seldom used (mainly because it isn't needed) unless we're dealing with attorneys here—**9**s make fantastic lawyers.

This may be because they are really, really smart.

The **9** naturally reaches a correct conclusion in about 30 seconds. This does not go for resolving problems. They could meet a problem lip to lip and still not recognize it as *being* a problem mainly because their philosophy seems to be that if they don't notice it, it will go away.

Under these circumstances, it is not surprising that a **9** has a rather turbulent married life *if* they marry (the

Virgo **9** is considered to be a natural loner in numerology.)

If, however, they do assume the responsibility of wedlock (or any other partnership) they are true and faithful companions. This doesn't mean they will wax sentimental over anniversaries, birthdays, childbirth, or Christmas; it only means that they will be there for these occasions—if possible.

Philanthropic activities are natural to a **9**. They really do care and want to help others. As soon as this is known about them, there is a steady stream of petitioners—all with a worthier project that needs them.

Almost indefatigable, a **9** will work until they get the job done, but they must want to do it. Otherwise, hell, high water, or piteous pleading will not get them to fix the kitchen sink or iron those shirts.

Friendships are selectively made (and kept) despite arguments that can crop up if they disagree. Generally speaking, people learn early not to disagree with a **9**—life is too short as it is.

The good part is: a **9** may be testy but is never petty.

Some **9**s seem to be extraordinarily involved in fires and accidents. They also experience more surgery than most other numbers (possibly because of that quick temper.)

Being a number of culmination, the **9** is revered by the Ancients as being "lucky". In view of the tendencies towards accidents, fires, and fights, perhaps they felt that a **9** was lucky to just be alive!

The Meaning of Your Particular 9 Birthday

9

With an active mind and the ability to easily solve the New York Times crossword puzzles, these **9**s are truly superior people.

Being well-liked is essential and they will do anything to get approval—rescue kittens and babies from burning buildings or race a football from one goal post to the other without touching the ground. Mediocracy is not tolerated. This goes for themselves as well as for others. But they should try to stop contradicting others. If someone says a cow is black, don't say it is white—even if the cow *is* white!

18-9

This number wants to be the boss. And is determined to succeed no matter what the obstacles may be.

A natural hero, the **18-9** will come a'runnin' if someone is in trouble. They are also daring. A certain **18-9** I know flew his transport plane under the Golden Gate Bridge and had no trouble finding Amelia Earhart's lost Howland Island in the middle of the Pacific ocean.

Since they seem to attract a bit of treachery and deception, they need to keep an eye on so-called friends. Ignoring warning signs (that moving van parked at the back door, for instance) can bring loss.

Also, they should be wary around the elements. For some reason, an **18-9** can find that tree in the middle of the road, a defective firecracker, or a leaky boat faster than anyone else.

27-9

This **9** has a smoother journey through life than other **9**s. Those who have this number will reap benefits based on what they learn in this lifetime—unlike other numbers who reap from talents and abilities begun in past lives.

Intellect combined with good looks and the ability to meet all obstacles with fortitude and authority is a hallmark of this super number. Which may be why they have no trouble with new puppies, in-laws, or shopping malls.

14

A Rose by Any Other Name

If your name number isn't in harmony with your birthday, you're swimming upstream against the tide; and unless you're a salmon looking for someplace to spawn, why do it?

We're only talking about the name you answer to when called and use whenever you sign a check, charge card slip, citation, or I.O.U.

For those who have long felt uncomfortable with their name, it is probably because that name is out of sync with the birthday numbers. Harmony can be accomplished by changing the spelling, adding or dropping an initial, or—if you really hate being called Gertrude or Clarence—changing it altogether; call yourself Milly or Steele. Just be sure the new numbers fit in with your birthday.

Here is a handy guide: the **3, 6,** or **9** mesh with each other. The **1, 2, 4, 7,** and **8** are in harmony. These groups would just as soon not be intermixed—the **3s** with the **4's,** etc (**5**s get along with any number!)

This is why a **4** birthday with a **3** name would be happier with a name number from its own group. And **3s** will stop feeling like the misfits of the world if they change from a **4** name to a cozy **3, 6,** or **9.**

A bit of advice to the **4**s and **8**s. Try not to strengthen your karmic vibrations! **8s** using an **8** name can do very well. Ditto **4**s. It's interchanging them that seems to bring conflict—maybe. As mentioned before, they're unpredictable. Margaret Truman, only child of President Harry S Truman (May **8**th), was born Feb.**17** with a **4** first name, a **4** last name, and a **4** keystone letter (the letter T). Her total name adds up to the **8** of her birthday. She had a happy childhood, successful singing career, good marriage, and is a best-selling author of mystery books. Incidentally, her mother, Bess Truman, was also karmic, born Feb.**13**. (Whew!)

I give you both sides of the picture because I want you to become as confused as possible when dealing with karmic ties and end up calling everybody born on a **4** or **8** day "Fred, baby".

It takes about six weeks after a name change for the new vibration numbers to take effect. During that time, write the new name as often as possible: checks, doodling, walls…(just kidding). Most states do not require a legal name change and won't object unless your previous name is featured on a Wanted poster in the local Post Office. Check it out with your Motor Vehicle Department. They will tell you pronto if you can use the new name legally.

And now—Ta DAH!—here is the Fadic numbering system.

A	B	C	D	E	F	G	H	I	J	K	L	M
1	2	3	4	5	8	3	5	1	1	2	3	4

N	O	P	Q	R	S	T	U	V	W	X	Y	Z
5	7	8	1	2	3	4	6	6	6	5	1	7

15

Initially Speaking

You have a **Cornerstone** and a **Keystone** letter which you probably haven't given a single thought to unless you were getting tattooed or having your linens monogrammed.

The **Cornerstone** letter is the first letter of the name you are using (first, preferred, or nickname) and is an indication of tendencies to behave in a certain manner.

If it is a **1**, there is a tendency to be aloof, private, and independent; a **2** brings compliance and being a good sport; the **3** gives a sense of fun and love of beauty; the **4** acts as a restraint; a **5** inclines toward the unexpected; a **6** likes to be cozy, sociable; the **7** favors intrigues, religion, and the occult; and the **8** helps to keep spending in line.

The **Keystone** letter is the **first** letter of your **surname** *at birth* and has a prominent place in your numberscope as a sign post.

If it vibrates harmoniously with the day of birth, then this is the number of a person who has returned to his former family.

If it is at odds with the birthday number, then we are looking at a person who has returned ahead of time and is probably out of sync with their ordained incarnation cycle.

If it is in harmony with the day of birth but the name numbers aren't, then we are looking at the quick (or fairly quick) return of a member of the family whose life was cut short.

16

Your Balance Number

So, what about *other* initials in a name? Many a wee babe has been saddled with more names than Queen Victoria ever thought about giving to her offspring (Edward Albert David Eugene etc., etc., etc....!)

Or how about the fact that you haven't been using the name Suzy Glotz since your first wedding four marriages ago?

Simple. In the case of Royals, most simply answer to the name of Prince. And Suzy will use the name she currently signs on her alimony checks.

Most people use a first and last name but some add a middle initial (or maybe more—like *C.K.Dexter Haven*). In any event, *all* initials of the names used are called *Balance Letters* and will furnish the **Balance Numbers.**

Hillary Rodham Clinton, who may soon revert to using just Rodham again as she did before her election to the Presidency, is a good example. Her Balance Letters are H.R.C. which add up to a 10-**1** (H is a **5,** R is a **2,** and C is a **3. 5+2+3**=10-**1.**) This gives us her a Balance Number of **1**. So simple. (By the way, which came first? Hillary's dad? Or was *his* mother's name Rodham, too? Just wondering.)

Your Balance Number and What It Means

1—Adds the quality of independence but there could also be a streak of wanting to dominate others. You might want a change of initials if the **1** is already prominent in your numbers or you could be lonely.

2—Helps hold the line if you are inclined to be flamboyant or boisterous. If you are timid or ill-at-ease, this number needs to be changed.

3—Adds a love of beauty and sense of fun. An otherwise drab personality could be the belle (or beau) of the ball. Just don't let it fritter away too much time.

4—Steadies a skittish personality. If you are already so steady people need to check to see if you're still breathing, change an initial.

5—Sexy. This number could put a little spark into life. On the other hand, if you already spend a lot of time browsing through the *Victoria Secrets* catalogue or think that *Belle Watling* had a lot more fun than *Scarlett O'Hara,* then this balance number is not for you.

6—Congeniality and goodwill are your hallmark (*Santa Claus* has the **6** balance number). However if already reticent, this number could cool you down to levels of frostiness just above freezing—okay if you live in an igloo, but not so good for people who haven't acted on an impulse since they voted for Ross Perot.

7—Puts a brake on being impulsive. It isn't so great for those who have a tendency to blame everybody, including the cat, for the fact that they aren't rich, famous, and/or gorgeous.

8—This balance number acts as a prod, jarring your id to the point of thinking that nothing is impossible. If you are already inclined to be a teensy bit pushy, get a calmer number.

9—This number tends to stiffen your resolve if you're inclined to have trouble making up your mind about anything.

And now, just for fun, add up the initials of some people you know (or know of) and see how close they come to these interpretations. I'll give you a hint: Bill Clinton has a **5,** Hillary has a **1.** Al Gore a **4,** Marilyn Monroe and Doris Day an **8,** and Richard Nixon a **7.**

17

How to Find Your Destiny Path

Everyone—and thing—has a Destiny Path. When people, dogs, cats, events, meetings, projects, trips—even ideas—are born, governing vibrations are set into motion. In order to identify these vibrations, someone got the bright idea of numbering them. Voila! By knowing what the numbers mean, we can look at the date of birth of *anything*, add all the numbers up, and see the projected outcome—or path of Destiny. Is this neat or what?

A word of caution: you will probably be figuring Destiny Paths of various celebrities, and in the process, discover that Princess Diana, JFK, his son John Kennedy, Jr., and Marilyn Monroe all had the same destiny path number. The 16-7 is a powerful number that warns against throwing caution to the winds.

They key word here is "warns". We *do* have free will and the ability to use our numbers with a bit of common sense. Princess Diana seemed to go out of her way to tweak Royal noses; John, Jr. seemed not to understand the word "caution"; Marilyn Monroe didn't comprehend that cute as she was, a little tact was needed in dealing with some of her powerful paramours; and JFK threw caution to the winds in the face of threats by refusing to use the bulletproof "bubble" on his convertible.

So, what do you do if *you* have the very same number? Well, first, congratulate yourself on having a powerful destiny path; one that, if used wisely, can take you to the heights. Then, understand that a few soul lessons will come to the fore that need to be met with a modicum of common sense.

Just remember, quite a few *other* people were born on the very same day as each of the above individuals and I seriously doubt that they met the same type of fate. This could be because that same destiny path also means very, very old age.

The important thing is to use your destiny path number the way you would a road map. If detours are shown, do a little veering.

To find your *Destiny Path* number, add the **month, day**, and **year** of birth together, then *reduce to a single digit.* (The compound number shows the hidden meaning of the single digit.)

Here's an example: For **Aug. 28, 1947**, add the month (**8**), the day (**28**) and the year of birth (**1947**). It will add up to **1983;** add **1+9+8+3** and get **21-3**. This clues you in right away that nothing will come easily; the "21-**3**" means "Brilliant success after a long series of trials.

18

Destiny Path Numbers and Their Meanings

1—There is a lot for you to learn in this incarnation but you are going to want to be the boss. Try to remember that you must first learn to walk before you can take off on any highflying schemes.

2—You will be asked to follow others but this won't bother you. If you feel in the mood to pioneer, you will still follow the beaten path. Tact and diplomacy are innate with inner peace as your goal. This can even be extended to foreign shores. A born diplomat.

3—You could be the *Goodtime Kid* of all times! A gift of gab plus a genuine affection for your fellowman gives you the ability to get along with almost anybody. There is also a creative talent present. Use it.

4—You will work for anything you get. Left-over problems, relationships, and duties from a former life present themselves for payment this time around. The important thing is to not avoid any of them. Financial security is almost inevitable.

5—Be prepared for changes almost from day one. There will be many opportunities to change jobs, partners, towns, states, or even countries. Life won't be dull but there could also be a tendency towards accidents. A little caution is needed.

6—You will be relied on to adjust, clear up messy situations, assume responsibilities, be a mediator, and organize whatever needs organizing—whether it be a labor conference or a wedding reception. Lucky you.

7—Travel could be a big part of your life. You'll seek solace by or on large bodies of water and will prefer to be alone rather than mingle with groups of people. Languages come easily. So will interest in either the occult or religion.

8—Money, fame, or notoriety might possibly be yours—or karmic challenges that are surprising to say the least. This is a good business and economic number if you don't get too greedy. Because it is a karmic number, there is no cut and dried path. Good luck.

9—You can complete undertakings that have eluded you for several previous lifetimes. The success inherent in this number is mainly due to your own hard work; the efforts of others won't really count. At some point in time, you will finally decide to wind up a lot of things that have been bothering you for years.

10-1—New Beginnings arise throughout life. This is a veritable "Wheel of Fortune" with success and failure inherent throughout the life span. Since it promises that your plans will be carried out, it should be obvious that you plan carefully.

11-2—Stress will be your middle name so watch your health. The purpose of this number is to push an otherwise laid-back soul to the utmost of its ability. Many people of enduring fame, achievement, and popularity have this number for their Destiny Path. Bob Hope, the indefatigable entertainer of stage, screen, and war zones, is a classic example. Both his birthday *and* destiny path are an 11-2! (Wow!)

12-3—You could be a victim of other people's plans somewhere along the line so always be aware. There will be a tendency to worry about everything so try to be a little selective in what worries you. The good news is delightful and adoring friends, multiple talents, and good looks.

13-4—This indicates many tests passed in former lives and it is now time to reap. But, be careful! This number is powerful when used for the good of others and tacky when used for personal gain at the expense of others. Talents galore come with it so enjoy.

14-5—This number brings restlessness and a desire to see just how green the grass is on the other side; if not careful, you can fritter all your time away on a variety of places, jobs, and people. Good for business and money. Just watch the elements! There could be danger.

15-6—Social ties, good partnerships, and money are the hall marks of this sociable number. Superb communicators, drama is a natural milieu as is art, music, and ukelele playing. There could also be a bit of chicanery—the *Brooklyn Bridge* was probably first sold by a **15-6**— so always be on the up and up.

16-7—This number so often brings fame, popularity, great success, and long life that the recipient may grow careless and undo all the goodies. Try to be aware each day of the bounty heaped on you and act accordingly.

17-8—Fame, Money, and/or Notoriety seem to be associated with this number. Since it is one of those karmic numbers, however, life will be what you make it. This is true of all numbers but it holds doubly true for the **8**s and **4**s. Since there is plenty of talent, it should be fun.

18-9—A good business sense prevails but there will be urges to spend now, pay later—much to your regret. Outbursts could cost you a lot so learn early to keep that temper in check because you can win the admiration and affection of whole groups of people. There could be danger from the elements so let others set off the fireworks.

19-1—This number promises success, happiness, and esteem but says very little about its predilection for wavering back and forth, up and down, and forcing you to start over again just when you thought you had finally gotten the knack of things. Plan for the future but expect changes to occur.

20-2—Service to others is the main goal. A lot of good things happen because there are people in the world with this destiny path. Doctors, lawyers, Peace Corps workers, ambulance drivers, and actors all share this destiny path. They also share the delays and hindrances it brings.

21-3—Brilliant success is supposed to come after a long series of trials. The trick is to still be standing after just a few of those trials. Although failure might be brushed off like a piece of lint, a few lessons learned should serve as guides for future undertakings.

22-4—Operating under the theory that stupidity is a virtue seems to be the *modus operandi* for this number. Poor judgment leads to failure and/or disappointment if care isn't taken to carefully examine all "sure-fire" deals. Since it is one of the Master Numbers in numerology, it can be surprisingly, outrageously successful! Enjoy.

23-5—Great success comes with a little help from people in positions of power. It also guarantees protection from high powered individuals (I don't think this applies to the IRS, though!). It is a dynamic number, fraught with excitement and fun, but warns of sudden changes!

24-6—People just love you when you have this number and they can't do enough for you. You gain—big-time—through the opposite sex. Very similar to the **23-5**

(except it isn't so volatile), life is much smoother. Friends, friends, and more friends are happy additions.

25-7—Success comes from what is learned in this lifetime. It promises authority and power and money and happiness. Of course, if you have authority, power, and money, what's not to be happy? Because it is a **7**, spiritual beliefs run deep, acting as a guiding rod.

26-8—Watch out for bad partnerships and bad advice. Money-making ideas will spring forth. The trick is holding on to them—or the money. It *is* an **8**, one of those karmic numbers that will brook absolutely no hanky-panky but it certainly can bring you the goodies!

27-9—Power and the ability to carry out one's plans just flow from this number. Superior intellect prevails no matter what level you're on— you could be the smartest chimp in the zoo. There is fulfillment of long range goals, a winding up of lingering relationships, and success. If the temper is held in check, partnerships can last for years and years.

28-1—There is a promise of great success, but if care is not taken, all could be taken away. Because the **28-1** is so clever and has so many good ideas, opposition and competition seem to hover over this number like flies at a picnic. Does this bother the **28-1**? You bet it does but not enough to get it down. A very superior—if ever changing—life path!

29-2—This isn't easy but then nobody promised you a rose garden—or did they? Hard work, trials, and health problems do a lot of lurking but then so does fabulous success, recognition, and loyal friends. This number acts as a prod for an otherwise sluggish id. And—like spinach —it's good for you!

30-3—Esoteric choices take precedence over material things, isolating this little dreamer from a heartier, more realistic world. There is a surprising determination to reach goals—some of which seem to be concocted in Never-Never land—but they invariably succeed. Good looks, a quiet sense of fun, and musical talents abound. Very nice.

31-4—Self-contained, independent, and charming. Stubborn, emotional, and full of fun. If there is a chance to help the underdog, they'll be there. If *they* are the underdog, they'll find a way to help themselves. Although this is a karmic destiny path, it's powerful!

The rest of the numbers are simply repetitions of the above, ad infinitum. After all, a **4** is a **4** is a **4** is a **4** etc....

19

How to Find Your Personal Forecasts

Numerology is so much more accurate than the daily Horoscope columns. Wondering if any shred of that particular day's forecast applies to you personally is a thing of the past. You no longer need to know your "Sun Sign"; all you need to know is what month and day you were born.

In the first place, the sun sign is *not* the correct indicator of who you are; your *rising* sign is—the planet that was peeking over the horizon at the instant you saw the light of day. And the only way of knowing that sign is to know the exact moment of birth—which is why early Astrologers, fearing that their science was about to fall by the wayside, decided to make it easier for people by figuring "signs" according to the month they were born. Accordingly, "Leos" might really be "Aquarians", "Virgos" might be "Leos", and "Geminis" might actually be Pisceans"!

Happily, your personal numbers are available for consultation whenever you want them; it doesn't matter whether you know where or what time you were born— or if that was Eastern Standard Time, Pacific Standard

Time, Daylight Savings Time, or Greenwich time (a little village apparently smack dab in the middle of the world).

By using your birthday numbers, it's instant gratification!

You may be in a **3** personal year, Uncle Ralph in an **8** personal year, and it may be a **2** personal year for your boss. This *personal year* number then puts each one into a *different month* number with *different daily* numbers vibrations.

This means that even if you all have the same sun sign—and the same daily horoscope reading—you will actually have *different* vibrations and, therefore, different experiences.

There is no longer a need to start frothing at the mouth when your Daily Forecast—based only on your sun sign— predicts that "Leos are due for fun today"— while you are miserable with a bad head cold or have just been indicted for misplacing the company's assets.

The formula is easy and once learned, you'll never again have to wonder what day it is! Just remember: *reduce to one digit and drop the zeroes!*

Your new *personal year* always starts on January 1st and it affects each month, and therefore each day of that year. Here's how it works:

To find your *personal year,* first find your *key* number by adding month and day of birth together (for someone born on Aug. **5** add **8 + 5.** This totals 13-**4. 4** is the *key* for this birthday.)

Add this *key* number (**4**) to the current year to get your *personal year* number. (**4 + 2000 = 6**) **6** is the *personal year.* Remember to reduce to one digit and drop the zeroes!

Now that you know what *year* you are in, go for the *month*!

Add your *personal year* number to what ever month you want to know about. In this case let's take February. Add your **6** personal year to the **2**nd month. (**6 + 2 = 8**) February, therefore, is an **8** *personal month* for you.

To find your *personal day* number: Add your **8** *personal month* to the day. For Feb. **10**th—which is a **1** day— add **8 +1 = 9.** Your *personal day* is a **9.**

20

What to Expect From Your Personal Year Number

1 Year—This is the beginning year of a nine year cycle. You will definitely be thinking of starting off in a new direction—especially in September. Since our karmic wheel usually turns in 9 year cycles, it takes several years for the tide to turn. If things have not been so great, look forward to better times coming. On the other hand, if things have been super, start hedging your bets, dotting all the "I's" and crossing all the "t's". Just don't be too pedantic; by resisting the urge to fly off in a new direction, you may certainly secure your place in the world—but you may also miss out on something really wonderful.

The people you acquire as friends in a **1** year will be with you for the entire 9 year cycle unless you decide otherwise. Dec. 31st will be the deadline for terminating any relationships that you would rather not keep. Be positive. July will be the most memorable month of the year.

2 Year—This is a follow-up to what you started in your personal **1** year. It can be a lot less hectic than last year when you scrambled to get something new started. Now, you can take the time to look around, smell the flowers, and decide if this new direction is really the way you want to go. Opportunities present themselves when you least expect it and money should come when you need it. The main thing is to watch your health and don't let depression creep in—especially in September.

You may be a bit eager to believe whatever is fed into your receptive little ears so reconsider those "almost too good to be true" propositions before taking action. June is the prominent month for this year.

3 Year—A good year for creative enterprises. Paint the house, redo the living room, buy a new car, or get that tummy tuck. It is also a time for marriage. For some reason, when the **3** personal year hits, many a reluctant bride or bridegroom hits the aisle.

There is a tendency to fret—about little things; the big things you take care of easily. Just be careful that you don't fall victim to other people's plans.

As the karmic wheel turns, this third year of your nine year cycle will be the beginning of either an upward or downward trend. For this reason, carefully evaluate signs. If they appear to be negative, start taking steps to reverse what is happening. Really successful people seem never to have a down side to their cycles. This is because they beat 'em to the punch. May could be an important month in this respect.

In the meantime, entertain, try a new hairstyle, explore Art galleries, have a little fun—especially in September.

4 Year—You're ready to tackle all the things that were pushed to a back burner—luckily, you're in the mood to do it! Organizing things is a snap; new routines are welcomed; hunting for bargains becomes a game. Efficiency—with a capital E—is your middle name! Just make sure this applies to your bank balance; money is harder to come by so think twice before you run out and buy that spiffy convertible you've always wanted.

Trying to settle up old accounts for a past grievance isn't a good idea in a 4 personal year. For some reason (karmic?), things just don't turn out the way you think they should. And don't change jobs—you might not find another one for awhile. April is a month to remember.

5 Year—Changes can come out of the blue! The key word is to be adaptable, go with the flow and be ready to accept challenges. Things may start out on a rocky footing but before the year is over, things can really be great. There could be travel, a shift of scene, promotions, and unusual opportunities.

There may also be a strong urge for you to take matters into your own hands. Don't do it! If you leave a job, you may not find another one for quite a while. If you move from one residence to another, you will move again before the year is over. And, be warned: if you are a fire sign, be careful around fires; if an air sign, think twice before flying; if a water sign, wear your water wings; and if an earth sign, stay away from mountain climbing and downtown Los Angeles. This goes especially for the month of September. (March is interesting.)

6 Year—This can bring a partner or take one away. The **6** stands for a joining or separation; marriage or divorce; birth or death. You will more than likely find yourself signing contracts or papers of some kind—especially in September. Other than that, the year could be more companionable and more sociable than usual. People who have been out of your life for sometime could return and friendships can resume as if they had never been interrupted. Opportunities to socialize are on the horizon and—if you're single—this can be the time to find a partner.

Then, again—it could be just the opposite; you could find yourself more alone than you've ever been. (Don't you just love the fact that there are always two sides to all the numbers in numerology? Well, anyway, February stands out and November ain't bad!)

7 Year—You could be traveling to places that would have been out of reach before—and there will probably be a large body of water nearby! This is also a time to take stock of your situation and maybe think of yourself for a change. Spiritual matters are on your mind and you might find that you prefer to be alone. On the other hand, since this year can bring an unexpected, blazing hot romance into your life, your urge to be alone could be short-lived.

It is a time for evaluating what is important and rectifying matters that may have slipped into disrepair—the true values of relationships come into focus. If there are setbacks of a personal or financial nature and health problems crop up, don't let it get you down. Work opportunities are there. Just don't overdo in the pursuit of the Buck! September could be the flash point month; January a stand-out month; and October an important money month!

8 Year—If you are an **8,** then this year could be a roller-coaster year. Expect the unexpected. Feast or famine. Fame or infamy. Just don't expect the *expected!*

For *normal* (non-karmic) numbers, this can be the time when all your efforts finally come home to roost. Financial matters are favored, recognition of your efforts could finally happen, and—who knows?—you could possibly win the lottery. (September?)

This is a time to seek out influential people who might help with a project you can't get off the ground— or can recommend you for that really spectacular job— just don't forget to say "Thank you".

Here's the bottom line: an **8** year can be a grab-bag of tricks or treats. And you don't have to wait until October to find out.

9 Year—This is one of those years. Hard to get through in some cases because you are finishing up a nine-year cycle and all the tag ends are clamoring to be taken care of. Just take things as they come and do the best you can. It can be a very exciting time as some old situations are ended and new ones begun. Projects you have been working on for the entire nine year cycle could bear fruit—hopefully, not lemons.

This is the time to get rid of things—or people—that have been bugging you. Fussing with stuff you don't want around uses up time that could be spent on some-thing you enjoy—so call the Salvation Army and give it to them. As for idle acquaintances who apparently have nothing better to do than to bug you, be sweet but be firm.

Try not to consider committing hari-kari because, by September, the year could bring some surprising results to all your efforts. You might actually get something you've long wanted—that new SUV or tickets to a John Tesh concert. By the way, August is the most memorable month.

21

What to Expect from Your Personal Month Number

1 Month—New beginnings. It's time to go after what you want! It may be a new idea, a new job, moving into a new home, getting that long awaited puppy, or an urgent desire to cut off all your hair. It could also be a time for standing alone.

2 Month—This is the time to follow through on whatever was started in your **1** month (get a wig maybe?) Tact is necessary as you mend any relationships that might have been jeopardized previously. Watch out for a germ or two. If sniffly, stay out of drafts.

3 Month—This can be a very pleasant time. Social get-togethers as well as some really good shopping can happen. On the other hand, keep alert for a bit of duplicity but don't make mountains out of mole hills.

4 Month—Time to take care of things that have been put aside. Clean the house, fix the car, pay off lingering bills—or at least seriously contemplate doing those things. If you vibrate to the **4** (**2 or 7**) this could be a pleasant month. If not, it could still be a pleasant month.

5 Month—Keep your wits about you and expect the unexpected. It can be a very exciting month if you keep your emotions in hand—they could run the gamut from very, very low to the skies! If there are upsets, don't take them too seriously. They can be resolved next month. And watch your driving—or other people's driving! Be careful.

6 Month—You could be signing contracts, a bill of sales, marriage licenses, or divorce decrees. There could be a new baby or the loss of someone near and dear. It also brings pleasant social interludes. The **6** governs things coming into your life and things leaving. Interesting.

7 Month—Trips, water sports, occult studies, religious debates, or an overpowering urge to be alone: take your pick! Since the **7** seems to bring a "red-hot romance" to some, you could also meet "The One and Only". I guess it all depends on which Starbucks you hang around the most.

8 Month—This could be the most memorable month of the year for you. Boldly going where no one has ever gone before or simply hitting it big in the stock market could all happen in an **8** personal month. Important decisions could be made, losses could occur, and long-term relationships could be jeopardized. This is not the time to issue ultimatums. (Actually, no time is a good time for that!)

9 Month—Endings are uppermost which could mean the completion of a project or finally deciding to go on that diet. You could get rid of things and/or get new ones. And someone you haven't seen in years could reappear.

22

What to Expect From Your Personal Day Number

1 Day—A good day to start something. It could be a new job or the urge to start house-hunting. In any event, don't fret if you find yourself having to repeat things.

2 Day—Follow up on what you started yesterday. If it's a bad head cold, just take it easy. Today is mostly busy work (or blowing your nose).

3 Day—Great day to go shopping. Bargains just seem to pop up! See friends or at least give them a call; a good phone chat can do wonders. Try not to stew over some little set back.

4 Day—It's nose to the grindstone time. Oh, well, those nagging little problems have to be met sometime so you may just as well do it now. Mow the lawn, clean the house, tackle those bills. It can be fun.

5 Day—Changes are in the air. Routines are interrupted. You might even decide to try that new hair style that looks as if it were cut with a machete. Just be careful. This is an accident prone vibration.

6 Day—*Getting to Know You* could be your theme song today. Enjoy friends but don't get into any arguments— you could lose one. In any event, papers may be signed.

7 Day—Travel or stay at home with a good book. The occult—or religion— may intrigue. If there is an unex- pected romantic encounter, be wary. In any event, plans may go awry—so hang loose.

8 Day—A good money day. Ask for that raise or buy a lottery ticket. Who knows? At least it won't be dull— especially if you happen to be an **8.** In any event, expect the unexpected.

9 Day—Don't get into any arguments and try not to lose anything. You may not find it again. This is a good day for finishing rather than starting (unless you decide to stop smoking and start being healthy.)

So there you have your own handy-dandy little method for finding out just what the day's vibrations will be. You can, of course, check out chapter seventeen and delve more deeply into these numbers, adding addi- tional interpretations as to what the year, month, or day will bring. You can even look at the harmonious versus inharmonious vibrations as it relates to your number. But frankly my dears, keep it simple.

23

Your Lucky Number —and How to Find It!

To explore whether or not the numerological vibrations of a certain day will be favorable for something you want to do, try this method followed by a lot of nervous don't-want-to-take-any-chances people.

Add up the total number of the name(s) you use every day.

Now add that number to your birthday.

Add that number to the day in question.

Now look up the meaning of that number and see if it in holds any optimism for you.

Lets say your name is Fred Smith (forget the fact that you will be called by your first name all the time unless waiting in your doctor's or the employment office.)

F r e d S m i t h adds up to a **9** ("Fred" is a **1** and "Smith" is an **8**)

8+2+5+4   3+4+1+4+5

(19-**1**)   (17-**8**)

Now let's say that Fred was born on November **3** and wonders what kind of a day December **23** will be. Fred will add his name number (**9**) to his birthday (**3**) to the day (**5**).

(**9 +3 + 5 = 17-8**)

The answer is: 17-**8**, an excellent money day.

Just for fun, see what Personal year, month, and day you were in on a few important days in your life. Were they "lucky"?

(Personally, I just check to see if my personal day is in harmony with my name. If so, I go for it.)

24

Other Destiny Paths

There are two more Destiny Paths involved with your numbers. One is your *Secret* Destiny Path which consists of your personal numbers on the day of birth. The other one is the *Universal* Destiny Path which consists of numbers in effect universally.

At this point, you may be thinking that three Destiny paths are a bit redundant—and you're right! The Secret and Universal Destiny paths are simply additional routes furnished by the AAA of the Soul.

So, without further ado, here is how to find them:

The Secret Destiny Path

1: Jot down your birthday numbers including your destiny path. (Aug. **8, 2000 = 8 + 8 + 2 = 18-9 Destiny Path**)

2: Add your destiny path to month of birth to get your personal number for that month. (**9 + 8 = 17-8 Personal Month**)

3: Add personal month number to day of birth to get your personal day. (**8 + 8 = 16-7 Personal Day**)

4: Add all three numbers (Destiny Path, Personal Month and Personal Day) together to arrive at your

Secret Destiny Path. (**9 + 8 + 7** = 24-**6 Secret Destiny Path**)

You can use Secret Destiny Path numbers to pick up clues as to who may have been who in a previous life, what other aspects may be hovering over your life, and what Secret number* is influencing your birthday. (* Your personal day number added to your actual day of birth.)

As you've no doubt noticed, I used only the single digits as I went along but used the compound numbers as my guide to what kind of a number I'm dealing with. This keeps things simple and doesn't drive you nuts trying to deal with compound numbers that have to be reduced and then reduced again to get the normal number reading.

The Universal Destiny Path

This destiny path deals with numbers in effect all over the world—or at least in your time zone.

1: Jot down the date of birth. (Aug. **8, 2000** = **8 / 8 / 2 2 is the Universal Year**)

2: Add the Universal Year number to the month to get the universal month number. (**2 + 8** = 10-**1 Universal Month**)

3: Add the Universal Month number to the day to get the universal day number. (**1 + 8** = **9 Universal Day**)

4: Add all three universal numbers together to arrive at the *Universal Destiny Path.* (**2 + 1 + 9** = 12-**3 Universal Destiny Path**)

As for the Universal Destiny Path numbers, I usually check to see if it is a Universal **5** day. If it is, I watch my

step and—if on the road—watch out for the other
fellow; people will be driving like maniacs!

You might figure some of the Universal Destiny Path
numbers for memorable dates in history. Could be
surprising.

25

Your New Birthday

Death dates give the date of return!

Really? you say, what about those plane loads of passengers who go down together? Or what about the Titanic? Do those people *all* come back on the same day?

The answer is yes—but not necessarily in the same year.

In order to find out just when they do return, follow this formula:

Jot down the date of the event then figure the three destiny paths because *the three destiny paths give the new birthday!*

For example: The Titanic sank on April 15, 1912.

This gave a *Regular* Destiny Path of 14-**5.**

The *Secret* Destiny Path was 20-**2.**

The *Universal* Destiny Path was a 17-**8.**

The Regular Destiny Path of the day of the event adds up to a **5.** This will be the regular destiny path of the new birthday.

The Universal Destiny Path adds up to a **17-8.** This tells us that **17**-8 will be the *day* of return (in this case, *do not* reduce to a single digit!)

The Secret Destiny Path gives us the *month* of return (a 20-**2**). You'll notice that a **2** month could be February or November. This is where the compound number helps: the 20-**2** stands for Service to Others, and the astrological sign seeking to serve others is Aquarius, an air sign.

Therefore, *February **17**, with a **5** Destiny path is the new birthday.*

To pinpoint the actual return year of the sudden, accidental passing of a youngster, add the age at death to the year of passing, then choose the closest year that gives the correct Destiny Path—in this case a **5**. For instance: a l6 year old goes down with the ship. Add **l6** to 1912 and you get 1928. In order to get a **5** Destiny path, you need two more years so move ahead to 1930—or go back to 1921 (a lot of youngsters who leave prematurely won't wait.)

Older people will either wait on the other side for members of their family to join them or they may decide to return immediately. Interestingly, they may also come back in a completely different sign. In this case, put down the month and day of projected return and estimate the future year based on what you know about the individual. If they are past the age of 50, they will probably wait for 30 or 40 years before returning.

Some souls are impatient—even if they have lived their four score—or more— years. Mark Twain was one of them. He passed away on April 21, 1910 but waited only 15 years on the other side before returning on February 17, l925.

(Twain's death date of April 21, 1910 had a **9** Destiny path, a 20-**2** Secret Destiny Path, and a 17-**8** Universal Destiny Path.)

Hal Holbrook, who has become famous for his Mark Twain one-man show, was born that very day!

(I know this is the same month and day as the Titanic's returnee date but Twain died two years before the ship sank and when I did Hal's numbers, he never once mentioned a fear of water to me.)

Twain adored giving lectures before large audiences during the last period of his fame. Hal, obsessed with Twain from childhood, started doing Twain's "lectures" in parks or coffee-houses when he was just into his teens. Coincidence? I don't think so.

26

Quickly Returning Souls!

Quickly Returning Souls usually wait on the other side for a period of a few months to 20 years, depending on how anxious they are to return—otherwise, we're looking at 99 years!

When lives are interrupted ahead of time, these "interruptees" usually come back to the family circle they left. The only thing "new" will be the body but they are usually *recognized* by a trait, resemblance, or even a talent.

These returnees always adore certain time periods. Babies born during and shortly after World War II—the "Baby Boomers"—can get nostalgic over the Big Band Sound, anything to do with World War II, or songs from the Twenties.

And many children born during or soon after the War were dyslexic—writing and reading from right to left. I feel certain that many are QRSs from the Holocaust.

Another interesting facet of QRSs is their affinity for people who are older than they are. This is because they would have been the same age if they had survived in their former incarnation. This may help explain those

May-December marriages. They knew one another previously.

Babies, returning after a previous traumatic death, are very sensitive to loud noises. A young man who was shot by a fleeing thief returned two years later to his family circle on the day predicted. The family was told that the child would react loudly to any unexpected noise. When the surgeon dropped an instrument on the delivery room floor and the baby howled, the family was ecstatic.

Some children find that they have either picked the wrong parents, or the wrong date to be born. They quickly leave in order to return on the proper date (or to more suitable parents for their particular incarnation). This is especially true for "karmies". Trying to get their "debts" paid isn't easy. They may be born in a wretched environment, physically afflicted, with parents who are less than supportive. This could incur future karma for the parents. It may even result in more bad karma for very person who is trying to get old accounts settled.

In cases like this, the *Over Soul*—the real you that has been trying on different bodies throughout the ages—terminates the situation. Too much bad karma can cause one to go into limbo for several lifetimes to recuperate spiritually.

Many QRSs, who left as the result of a disastrous occurrence—war, car or plane crash, drowning, etc.— want to get back as soon as possible and will join the first available family. When this happens, you are looking at someone born on a **5** day. Strangely enough, many of these **5**s are born to late-life parents and are an only child. The QRSs love these parents but never really know them.

If their previous passing had been violent, most QRS will have a memory it of until they are **8** or **9** years old. These flashbacks will usually occur just before they drop off to sleep. One child, born on Oct.**14,** would mutter "Save yourselves men, the sea is on fire" just before going to sleep at night. When he got older, he read everything he could find about the battleship Maine. Another little girl who was accidentally run over by her father's pickup truck, came back on the very day predicted—to her sister. She was very fearful of cars and when she could talk, warned "Be careful of the car, mommie." She also looked exactly like the little girl "lost".

When you jot down the birthday of someone and notice that their name number is out of kilter with the day they were born, this indicates a QRS who was formerly a member of their family.

QRSs who previously had sad lives—living until they were old, incapacitated, or abandoned before they died—are in a hurry to experience the joy they missed. They come back just months after that sad state. The next time you see a toddler squealing with glee while examining a daisy, take a second look. You could be looking at someone who has just started a new, much happier, incarnation.

Here's what to look for if you suspect you are dealing with a QRS:

Are the name numbers out of sync with the present birthday?

Check out the Secret Destiny path. Does the Secret birthday correspond with the present name numbers?

Does the cornerstone (first initial of last name) tally with the birthday? (A returning family member can have a name out of sync with the birthday but still have a cornerstone initial that meshes.)

This can be an interesting search but—for what it's worth—very few of you were ever Cleopatra or Marc Antony in a former life.

27

Advanced Birthdays

If you want to get really picky, you have another birthday occurring each year. But, unlike your real birthday—which is fixed and unchangeable—this New birthday does change each year. It even puts you into new astrological signs.

Here's how it works:

Lets say a **34** year old born on **Aug. 28, 1966** wants to know what her advanced birthday would be for the year **2000.**

Start on Aug. **28** and count **34 days.** This brings her to **Sept. 30.**

So her advanced birthday for that year is *September 30, 1966.* Now figure the destiny path of that date— even unto "personal" years, months, and days. Her sign also changed from Virgo to Libra. Now, not only will she be a workaholic, she'll weigh both sides of every question ad infinitum—or until her sign changes again when she reaches Scorpio.

Each astrological sign is in effect for approximately **29 days.**

One year of your life equals one day in that 29 day cycle.

So start counting starting with the day you were born and go forward, one day at a time. If you were born on August **8th**, then you were in the sign of *Leo* until your **15**th birthday. You would then enter the sign of *Virgo* (Virgo begins on Aug. **23**) and life would take on the characteristics of a Virgo for you. This brings new responsibilities—babysitting, washing dishes, or having to make your own bed. You would also start preferring silver instead of gold jewelry and wearing cooler colors.

So start counting!

In the spirit of being helpful, here are the 29 day cycles and their astrological signs:

Aries—March 21 to April 19 — (Fire)
Taurus—April 20 to May 20— (Earth)
Gemini—May 21 to June 21 — (Air)
Cancer—June 22 to July 22 — (Water)
Leo—July 23 to August 22 — (Fire)
Virgo—August 23 to September 22 — (Earth)
Libra—September 23 to October 22 — (Air)
Scorpio—October 23 to November 21 — (Water)
Sagittarius—November 22 to December 21 — (Fire)
Capricorn—December 22 to January 19 — (Earth)
Aquarius—January 20 to February 18 — (Air)
Pisces—February 19 to March 20 — (Water)

28

Why People Like People

When Lolita Lovely eloped with the plumber, people wondered what in the world she saw in him. He wasn't rich, famous, or even good-looking. But he did have something that was irresistible to her—his numbers linked up to her numbers!

Her *key* linked to *his* birthday number and his *key* linked to *her birthday.*

They had the same *Destiny Path* number

Their *total name number*s were the *same.*

And, they were both in a **3** personal year which, of course, is a Honeymoon year. (Did I mention that a lot of marriage-shy people marry in a personal **3** year?)

There are lots of reasons why people get married but many Love-At-First-Sight liaisons happen because of one or more of the above.

However, I would like to mention that they are usually also in compatible signs. Lolita was Gemini (**Air**) and the plumber was Leo (**Fire**).

In other words, their "signs" also complimented each other. (**Fire** and **Air, Water** and **Earth**). Two fires are too hot; two airs may spend more time talking than loving, and mixing fire and water puts out the fire. Whew!

Here is how it works:

There are four elements: **Earth, Air, Fire,** and **Water.** We all fall into one of these classifications. The common element is water because all new souls begin in this very basic sign. I will say at this point that advanced old souls who have elected to come back as Teachers will also start in a water sign. Just don't be surprised if a favorite genius has the same birthday as someone who hardly knows how to peel a banana.

The Ancients thought about how these elements work to bring harmony or cause friction in relationships and came to these conclusions:

Two Air signs never stop discussing things.

Fire and Water disagree—water puts out fire!

Earth and Water nurture one another.

Fire and Air get along because air makes fire burn.

Two Fires are never dull—sparks will fly.

Earth dampens Fire's ideas but gets along with Air.

Simple? Now check out that relationship that bugs you or delights you Here is a lineup that will help you determine just who is what.

Polarization Equals Harmony

EARTH	FIRE
April 20-May 20	March 21-April 19
August 23-September 22	July 23-August 22
December 22-January 19	November 22-December 21

AIR	WATER
May 21-June 21	June 22-July 22
September 23-October 22	October 23-November 21
January 20-February 18	February 19-March 20

Water is the beginning, basic sign; Earth follows; Fire is next, then Air is the final, ultimate sign.

29

Marriage Ground Rules

Marriage, under the best of circumstances, is a situation fraught with booby traps. ("Why does he insist on putting his shoes on the mantle?" or "I wonder what makes her think I like burnt pot roasts?") It is never easy because these are two people who were used to being single.

Today's partnerships are often preceded by a trial period—presumably to get to know and understand one another. This, of course, is a fallacy. Both are usually on their good behavior, diligently concealing any little flaws they may have until they say "I do". Afterwards, they find out how many "I don'ts" there are!

"Those whom God hath joined together, let no man put asunder" is a nice thought, but a good marriage destiny path (and no outside interference) helps. One thing to remember: a "good" marriage destiny path number is no guarantee if one of the partners uses the other one as a punching bag. The MDP may simply mean that they survive.

Incidentally, Destiny paths 1 through 9 are essentially the same as their compound counterparts. For that reason, I am giving only the stronger numbers which are *not* reduced to the final single digit.

30

Marriage Destiny Paths

Add month, day, and year of marriage, them check out the Destiny Path number to see if going home to mother is on the horizon.

10-1—This Destiny Path denotes power for the union. There will be a new beginning of some sort for this couple in the marriage's during the latter years— starting a new business venture, relocating to an Art Colony, taking up Ballroom dancing, or maybe just having the last kid leave home!

11-2—This marriage will be busy, productive, and "involved"—both could be in community service work, politics, medicine, teaching, or the arts. It is almost the same as having a **20-2** Destiny Path except there could be unusual problems and things could get a little tense.

12-3—Pleasure, gratification, and compatibility could lead to restlessness—after all, a steady diet of ice cream with no spinach could pall. One or the other may go home to mother. Just try not to fret.

13-4— This Destiny Path could denote having every-thing you both missed having in a previous incarnation. It also indicates that some Karma—good and/or bad—will be present.

14-5—A lot of traveling salesmen and politicians have this Marriage Destiny Path but absence doesn't neces-sarily make the heart grow fonder. Divorce is possible—long before the actual papers are filed.

15-6—There could be periods of adjustments to be dealt with but working together helps overcome any tendency to blame the other half. Happily, it brings help if you need it—and lots of friends!

16-7—This marriage could last until infinity but, although it's so powerful all your ambitions could be met, the number also warns of disappointment or an upset. Well, nobody promised you a rose garden.

17-8—This marriage could be affluent. It could also be noted for something else—being the messiest neighbors on the block or the husband/wife team who wrote the best seller on *Mating Habits of the Yellow-Bellied Sap Sucker.*

18-9—This one usually lasts if there isn't any decep-tion. It could also be the completion of a karmic rela-tionship. Watch out for carelessness that could lead to fires or accidents.

19-1—On again, off again. Up, down. Expect to have varied experiences with this "one." You could go from Urban living, complete with swimming pool, to life on a farm with only the cows and chickens to talk to, then back to urban living and an even bigger swimming pool.

20-2—This Destiny Path stands for service to others. You could wind up running a motel or become co-Presidents! In any event, it is almost certain you will both be helping others in a big way.

21-3—Brilliant success after a long series of trials for this Marriage. The trick is survive the "trials". (Let all of the in-laws stay home on the holidays!)

22-4—Deception is the keyword here. (It might turn out that her "36-24-36" figure is really "24-24-24 and he wears a toupee!) There is some Karma to be met jointly, but it won't interfere with having a long and happy union. Just watch those investments.

23-5—If you have a weak constitution, pick another date. This one is full of power plays, big changes, and sudden endings. There will be separations, accidents, and the years will be dotted with little cries of "oops"! It is almost a sure-fire urge for divorce. Wait a day.

24-6—There are adjustments to be made but assistance comes when you need it. Winning the lottery and giving up the trailer home for a fifteen room mansion isn't as far-fetched as it may seem.

25-7—This marriage gets stronger as it progresses. All those little prayers of "Give me strength" over starched socks and sterilized pipes are answered. (And, she will learn to live with exploding toasters, collapsing chairs, and erupting garbage disposals)

26-8—Motives may be questioned, but as long as you are true to each other, all will be well. A word of caution, temptation in the form of sure-fire investments or easy ways to make money could be disastrous.

27-9—This is a culmination number and indicates that lots of little problems will be resolved. Cooperation and joint efforts can bring satisfaction—to say nothing of plenty of money.

28-1—There may be terrific urges on both sides to spend money but this is a powerful number indicating more than one dynamic change of direction for the union.

29-2—There could be a lot stress throughout the latter part of the marriage with physical problems being uppermost. There will be a tendency, however, to work together as a team. (He will learn to eat—and to love—her tofu casseroles and she will decorate around his prized beer can collection.)

30-3—"Let me entertain you" could be this couple's theme song. On the other hand, they will be very happy spending quiet time with just their books and music.

31-4—Nothing will really come easily but when it *does* come, it could be the jackpot! Because this destiny path denotes karma from past lives, this one could be verrrry interesting and about as dull as a ride on a roller-coaster.

Marriage, like life, is what you make it. Look at the destiny paths of other marriages and see how they coped. Just remember, no two people will use their numbers the same way. That's why so many try, try again.

31

Hail to the Chief!

If you have double letters or the word "on" in your name, your chances of becoming President are greater than someone who doesn't—or so some numerologists have pointed out. During the late twenties and thirties, the double "O" was prevalent in presidential names. Lately, there has been a lot of "ons".

Here is a list of all 42 Presidents. The ones that "do" and the ones that "don't" are listed in order.

Double Letters or "On":	*Neither:*
George Washingt<u>on</u>	Martin Van Buren
J<u>oh</u>n Adams	James Knox Polk
Thomas Jeffers<u>on</u>	Zachary Taylor
James Madis<u>on</u>	Franklin Pierce
James M<u>on</u>roe	James Buchanan
J<u>oh</u>n Quincy Adams	Rutherford B. Hayes
Andrew Jacks<u>on</u>	James Garfield
Wi<u>ll</u>iam H. Harris<u>on</u>	Grover Cleveland
J<u>oh</u>n Tyler	Gerald R. Ford
Mi<u>ll</u>ard Fi<u>ll</u>more	George Bush
Abraham Linc<u>oln</u>	Chester Alan Arthur

Andrew Johnson
Ulysses Simpson Grant
Benjamin Harrison
William McKinley
Theodore Roosevelt
William Howard Taft
Woodrow Wilson
Warren Gamiel Harding
Calvin Coolidge
Herbert Hoover
Franklin D. Roosevelt
Harry S. Truman
John F. Kennedy
Lyndon Baines Johnson
Richard M. Nixon
Jimmy Carter
Ronald Reagan
Bill Clinton

Dwight D. Eisenhower

32

How Much Is That Doggie in the Window? (And What Is His Birthday?)

The pet you choose should have harmonious vibrations to your birthday number. If not, this could mean the difference between a pet that is a joy to have around or a little beast that will cause you to lie awake nights wondering why you ever wanted it in the first place.

If your numbers line up, there is a very good chance you will have a pleasant, long-term relationship. That scroungy creature with the near-together eyes and a nose that looks as if it were part Ardvark (we're still talking about pets here!), could become one of the dearest friends you'll ever be allowed to care for because your numbers are together.

Look for these birthday links for compatibility.

Same Destiny path as yours? Great. If not, look for the "Key". (Month and day added together).

Is it the same as your key?

Does Fluffy or Rover's key add up to your birthday number?

Does your key add up to your little Rover or Fluffy's birthday?

Any or all of the above will insure pleasant relations.

Bear in mind that the numbers don't have to be identical—just in the same grouping such as **1, 2, 4, 7**, and **8** or **3, 6**, and **9.** For those with a **5** key, they can wag their tails with just about anybody.

Now, in case you don't have the birthday of little Maribelle or Frank, just give them a name with a number that is harmonious with your birthday! (You will anyway, because that's the way we usually do it.) So simple.

33

Be It Ever So Humble There's No Place Like Home
—With the Right Numbers

Remember that house you liked so well? I'll bet the numbers were in perfect sync with your birthday—unless, of course you are a **4** or an **8**. And even then, it could have been one of the more interesting occupancies.

The **4**s and **8**s must be especially wary of moving into a house with a number that adds up to an **8** or a **4**. **8**s should avoid **4** addresses and **4**s should avoid **8** addresses. Of course, if you find a dandy little home with a swimming pool, three baths, and a fireplace that rents for little more than a mere bag of shells, but adds up to a **4** and you're an **8**, go ahead and rent it but keep the emergency telephone numbers handy.

8s and **4**s can go with their name number. The rest of you can lope along, matching the groups of **1-4, 2** and **7** or **3, 6, or 9**.

Now if you really want to drive yourself crazy, add up the numbers of the town and state you live in. Compatible? If not, try *especially hard* to live in a user-friendly house number.

34

A Game People Can Play

Just clear your mind of everything except the question you're asking then visualize that question until you see it clearly. As soon as you feel ready for the answer, put down the first four numbers—**1** through **9**—that come to mind. Next, look up each number's meaning as well as the total.

1: Start something new
2: Cooperate, follow through
3: Socialize, go ahead and buy it
4: Work for it, clear up a matter
5: Change direction, expect the unexpected
6: Sign papers. Join in or leave. Buy or sell
7: Travel. Think things over carefully
8: Go for it! Money and fame may be yours!
9: Finalize plans. Make up your mind

Remember to always reduce multiple numbers to a single digit.

Have fun.

35

And Now, a Word to the (I Hope) Wiser

There is so much more to learn about numerology than I've written down on these few pages.

There are triangles and triangles within the triangles and triangles within the triangles that are within the triangles. All with meanings as subtle as the different grey shades within a grey scale—important only if you plan on painting a masterpiece of a numerology chart.

There are significant number links to the planets, the Bible, historic events, Shakespeare, and Elvis. Figuring them out can give you something to do on those occasions when you find yourself absolutely alone and bored silly.

There is your entire life span—even unto the age of departure—in the date you were born. (And, no! I won't tell you how to find that because you will simply either scare yourself or others half to death—and, in any event, you'll probably be wrong!)

And then, of course, there are those systems that rely almost solely (or so it seems) on graphs, charts, and diagrams that could send you reeling in the direction of the nearest bar.

If you learn—and learn well—all the little formulas I've given here, you should be quite content. But, in the meantime, go to your local library and check out other books on numerology, reincarnation, and—best of all— karma.

This lifetime can be a lot better than the one before and a preparation for an even better one to come.

Really and truly!

About the Author

Jil Balie

Numerology became my abiding hobby after a friend introduced me to it via a flashy lady who wore blue eye-shadow and looked as if she had another profession on the side. Intrigued, in spite of her appearance, I decided to investigate this theory on my own. I've been investigating it ever since and not once have I felt the urge to wear blue eye-shadow. I have however, written a couple of books on numerology. The latest one, *numerology For nitwits*, delves into reincarnation, karma, and "quickly returning souls".

My first book, *How to Be Happy Altho You're an Eight!*, sold very well and led to an offer of a daily half-hour stint beginning at 7:30 each evening on the ABC Television network. After an impressive number of celebrities were lined up, a capricious FCC decided that this time slot should be returned to local programing.

Roll Call, the prestigious Washington, DC newspaper, invited me to write a weekly column which attracted offers from two syndicates. Loathe to predict the things they wanted to me to write about, I contented myself with numerous television and radio talk show appearances (Maury Povich and I got to be good friends) until I tired of predicting that the marriage between Charles and Diana was never going to work. (At no time did I mention that her numbers showed a tragic, early end.)

I have been asked to do the numbers on just about everything and everybody including a furtive call from a prestigious magazine who wanted me to do the numbers of a famous talk show host and a former CIA agent who was going into hiding for reasons he never explained and needed his name changed. His secrets—whatever they were—are certainly safe with me; not only have I forgotten his real name, I have no idea what new name I gave him. He's probably lurking about somewhere with his collar turned up and answering to the name of Egbert.

My only real claim to fame is chatting with Howard Hughes for three weeks without ever catching his last name. With this type of acute perception, I naturally turned to Media promotion as a means of earning a living. Happily, my clients didn't suffer too badly and some actually got national attention.

Born and raised in Dallas, Texas, my "career" actually began after service in the Navy as a Control Tower Operator, marriage to a Marine pilot, and four kids. Somewhere along the line, I got into television with a successful children's show that ran for three years, adopted a little girl from Brazil, then—after the kids left the nest and the loss of my husband in a plane crash—I headed for Washington, DC to help my brother get his small Mexican food restaurant started. This led to a stint at Ford's Theatre which led to Media promotion.

Finding myself with a little time on my hands, I've also written two other books that have absolutely nothing to do with numerology: *Soiree at the Grange*, a memoir of California Pioneers in the 1950s, and its sequel, *"The Edsel and I"*. (Instead of "Ma" and "Pa" Ingalls of *Little House* fame, we were closer to "Ma" and "Pa" Kettle of *The Egg and I)*.

As Belle Watling said to Rhett Butler: "I try to keep myself occupied."

www.ingramcontent.com/pod-product-compliance
Lightning Source LLC
Chambersburg PA
CBHW020252290526
45784CB00003B/1211